PRAISE FOR
Making Great Relationships

"Everyone is 'in' relationship all the time. But most of us do not know 'how' to be there, so often it feels like we are not. Rick Hanson, who has educated us all about the brain, now brings his thoroughness and accessibility to relationships. Anyone reading this book will know they are in the hands of a master, and we encourage you to trust the effectiveness of the many practices the author provides, if you want a 'great' relationship."

—Harville Hendrix, PhD, and Helen LaKelly Hunt, PhD, coauthors
of *Getting the Love You Want: A Guide for Couples* and
Making Marriage Simple: Ten Relationship-Saving Truths

"Have you ever found yourself wondering how a conversation just went so wrong? *Making Great Relationships* is a wonderful guide to helping us understand the way to speak up and listen more fully. Rick Hanson offers his experience and insight in each chapter, which can be taken individually or as a whole. One can take the Buddha's advice to take what you need and leave the rest, but there is so much good you might not leave anything!"

—Sharon Salzberg, author of *Real Change: Mindfulness to
Heal Ourselves and the World*

"This brilliant new book offers science-based tools to help you thrive in your relationships. In *Making Great Relationships*, Rick Hanson offers deeply practical instruction on how to befriend yourself, cultivate kindness, and communicate more skillfully, so you can get more of what you really want in all of your relationships."

—Nate and Kaley Klemp, authors of *The 80/80 Marriage:
A New Model for a Happier, Stronger Relationship*

"Rick Hanson has offered us a treasure of practical wisdom, guidance, and inspiration. His years of hard-won insight shine through these pages like the forgotten voice of an old friend or a loving grandparent. I can't recommend this book enough to anyone looking to improve their relationships."

—Oren Jay Sofer, author of *Say What You Mean: A Mindful Approach to Nonviolent Communication*

making great relationships

Also by Rick Hanson

Neurodharma: New Science, Ancient Wisdom, and Seven Practices of the Highest Happiness

Resilient: How to Grow an Unshakable Core of Calm, Strength, and Happiness (with Forrest Hanson)

Hardwiring Happiness: The New Brain Science of Contentment, Calm, and Confidence

Just One Thing: Developing a Buddha Brain One Simple Practice at a Time

Buddha's Brain: The Practical Neuroscience of Happiness, Love, and Wisdom (with Richard Mendius)

Mother Nurture: A Mother's Guide to Health in Body, Mind, and Intimate Relationships (with Jan Hanson and Ricki Pollycove)

making great relationships

Simple Practices *for* Solving Conflicts, Building Connection, *and* Fostering Love

Rick Hanson, PhD

HARMONY
BOOKS · NEW YORK

Published in the United States by Harmony Books, an imprint of
Random House, a division of Penguin Random House LLC, New York.
HarmonyBooks.com
RandomHousebooks.com

Harmony Books is a registered trademark, and the Circle colophon is a
trademark of Penguin Random House LLC.

Library of Congress Cataloging-in-Publication Data
Names: Hanson, Rick (Psychologist), author. Title: Making great relationships /
Rick Hanson, PhD. Description: New York : Harmony, 2023. | Includes index.
Identifiers: LCCN 2022026138 (print) | LCCN 2022026139 (ebook) |
ISBN 9780593577936 (hardcover) | ISBN 9780593577943 (ebook)
Subjects: LCSH: Interpersonal relations. | Self-realization. | Mindfulness
(Psychology)
Classification: LCC HM1106 .H3645 2023 (print) | LCC HM1106 (ebook) |
DDC 158.2—dc23/eng/20220613
LC record available at https://lccn.loc.gov/2022026138
LC ebook record available at https://lccn.loc.gov/2022026139

ISBN 978-0-593-57793-6
Ebook ISBN 978-0-593-57794-3

Printed in the United States of America

Book design by Andrea Lau
Jacket design by Kathleen Lynch/Black Kat Design

10 9 8 7 6 5 4 3 2 1

First Edition

For all my friends and colleagues,
for everyone I've ever worked with,
for all those who've taught me,
and for anyone anywhere who has compassion

Contents

making great relationships

Introduction

Most of our joys and most of our sorrows come from our connections with other people. Just about everyone wants to be in healthy, fulfilling relationships. But *how* to actually do this, at home and at work, with friends and relatives, with people you like—and perhaps some you don't? How can you handle conflicts, repair misunderstandings, get treated better, deepen a romantic partnership, be at peace with others, and give the love that you have in your heart?

Many of us feel stuck, even trapped in our relationships. Perhaps with a tricky coworker or a frustrating roommate, a co-parent who won't do their share, an estranged relative, an overly critical boss, or a spouse who's drifting away from you. It can seem hopeless.

But here's the good news: Thousands of scientific studies show that relationships are not given; they are *made*. This gives us the power to make them better—and I once heard a teaching story that tells us how:

An elder was asked what she had done to become so happy and wise, so loved and respected. She replied: "It's because I know that there are two wolves in my heart, a wolf of love and a wolf of hate. And I know that everything depends on which one I feed each day."

You may have heard a version of this story yourself. It is so hopeful! Every day, with what you think and say, you can gradually build up a sense of self-worth, compassion, and confidence inside, while also becoming more relaxed, patient, and effective with others.

As a psychologist, husband, and father—and as someone who was shy and awkward as a kid, and struggled as an adult in some relationships—I've learned what makes relationships go badly, and what you can do to make them go better. This book will show you fifty simple, yet powerful ways to communicate effectively in all kinds of settings, stand up for yourself, express your deep feelings, stay out of no-win quarrels, say (and get) what you want, resize relationships as needed, forgive others and yourself, take things less personally, feel truly loved—and much more. It's the distillation of many years of experience, and it holds everything I would want to give to anyone who wants to know how to grow good relationships, and even great ones.

It usually takes a good deal of time to change the world around you. Inner change can happen a lot faster. You can take the steps that are within your own power to heal old wounds, to find support and happiness in your relationships as they are, and to make them even better. These are the fundamentals of *any* relationship, and you can apply them in any setting. I've focused on their essence in short chapters that rapidly cover a lot of ground, and am sometimes blunt and direct, offering real-world lessons drawn from decades as a psychotherapist with couples and families. I'm writing from my own background—as a white, professional, older man—and will unavoidably leave out important perspectives and issues. Please adapt what I say to your own needs and situations.

In parts one and two, we establish the vital foundation of support for *yourself* and a warm heart for others. Parts three and four lay the groundwork for dealing with conflicts and challenging people. Part five explores effective communication in detail, including what to do when things get intense. Part six expands the scope of our relationships to our communities, to all of life, and to our whole beautiful world.

Each chapter stands on its own as a complete practice. While the chapters build on each other, it's fine to jump around to what's most useful to you at the moment. I'll occasionally mention research findings, and you can easily find references in my books *Hardwiring Happiness* and *Neurodharma*, as well as online. If you come across something you've heard me say elsewhere, you can explore it more deeply or skip ahead a bit. In the space here, I haven't been able to address the important topics of finances, sex, childrearing, cyberbullying, workplace harassment, or the ways that our relationships can be burdened by sexism, racism, and other kinds of prejudice. I use mainly gender-neutral language, such as *they* or *them*.

Every day gives us chances to learn and heal and grow. We just keep trying. You can relate to some chapters as aspirational, such as "Say What You Want" (chapter 43) or "Take Care of Your Side of the Street" (chapter 24). What's important is that you keep moving in a positive direction and don't feel you have to be perfect.

In these pages, you'll find many specific things you could do inside your mind or outwardly with other people. For simplicity, I state most of them as instructions—and feel free to ignore the ones that don't work for you. Some will seem easy and obvious, and others will take more effort and be an ongoing exploration. Find what's good for you, and it's fine to leave the rest.

You could read this book on your own, or together with another person to improve that relationship. This book is not therapy, or any substitute for professional treatment of physical or mental health conditions. I've tried to write it as if I were talking with a friend about a relationship to explore its key issues and offer ideas and tools that would be immediately helpful. I hope that you get a *lot* out of reading this book, and that whatever you gain will ripple into the world to benefit other people as well.

Part One

Befriend
Yourself

1

Be Loyal to Yourself

Some years ago my friend Norman and I were climbing a route on Fairview Dome in Yosemite National Park. I finished leading a steep pitch, set anchors at a small ledge, and belayed Norman as he came up. Suddenly he popped off a hold and fell backward with his arms flung wide and a shocked expression on his face. His weight yanked me downward but the anchors held and I braked his fall. He looked up with a bemused grin, jammed his hands back in the crack, and kept climbing.

He knew I'd catch his fall, and on another day I knew he'd catch mine. We were *loyal* to each other, although usually in less dramatic ways. We stayed alert for threats, listened with interest, appreciated wins, and sympathized with losses. He looked out for me and I for him.

Most of us are loyal to some other people. Yet how many of us are loyal to *ourselves*? How often do you give yourself the same kind of encouragement, support, and respect that you give to others?

In my experience, lots of people have trouble being loyal to themselves, at least in certain areas. Maybe they can stick up for themselves at work but in their personal relationships they feel that somehow they don't have the right to be on their own side. As a therapist, I'd often meet someone who was pretty unhappy, for understandable reasons, given their life history and current relationships. But they downplayed or dismissed how they felt, as if it were embarrassing or a personal fault. They kind of shrugged at their own pain. They could tell me what they thought they ought to do, but underneath it all they weren't moved to help themselves actually do it. To move forward despite our inertia and fears, we need a dogged, loyal commitment to our own welfare.

Being loyal to yourself is like being loyal to anyone else. You see the good in that person. You're a faithful ally, both compassionate and supportive. This stance, applied to yourself, is the foundation of every good action you might take on your own behalf. It's like a pilot light. If it's unlit, no amount of "gas"—including the things we'll explore that could improve your relationships—will make much difference. But when it's lit, anything is possible. When you're for yourself, your one wild and precious life—as the poet Mary Oliver put it—matters to *you*.

Being loyal to yourself doesn't mean being selfish. When you recognize what is truly best for you, you know that you must give in order to take, that you need to hold others in your heart for your own sake as well as theirs. Wise loyalty is clear-eyed, not blind. In order to help yourself, you need to understand what you could do better next time. (Perhaps in the spirit of Suzuki Roshi's comment to a group of Zen students: "You are perfect as you are . . . and could use a little improvement.") Wise loyalty to yourself sees the big picture and takes the long view—for example, helping you disengage from no-win quarrels with someone.

It feels really good when someone is loyal to you, and you can have much the same feeling when you're loyal to yourself. Imagine what could shift for the better in your relationships if you were consistently committed to your deep true interests, if you gave yourself emotional support during conflicts, if you had a strong sense of the value of your life each day.

How

A good place to start is to bring to mind the sense of being loyal to someone you care about. What's this experience like? You might feel warmhearted support and sturdy persistence on their behalf, while having an awareness of that person's inner being, with its vulnerability and preciousness. Know what it's like to be loyal to someone.

And then apply this attitude to yourself. You could imagine seeing that person and yourself seated in front of you, and say first to the other person and next to yourself: *I am loyal to you . . . I am going to stick up for you . . . I think about what's really best for you . . . Your life truly matters . . .* What does it feel like to say these things? Are some easy to say to the other person, but hard to say to *yourself*?

Next, try saying these things out loud and notice how that feels: *I'm not against others, I'm simply for myself . . . My needs and wants matter . . . I'm determined to do what's good for myself, even if it's scary . . .* You could make these general statements specific to particular issues, such as: *I am going to stick up for myself at work . . . My needs and wants matter in this family . . . I'm going to talk about that argument with my friend, even if it's scary . . .* Be open to your intuition about what might be emotionally moving and important to tell yourself.

Dealing with Blocks

As you go through this exercise, you're exploring some of the depths of your own mind. Notice what you find there, especially any hesitations, any sense that you're not allowed to get on your own side, any feeling that you don't deserve that kind of support. Blocks to self-loyalty are common, notably:

- Beliefs that it's somehow "against the rules," that it's selfish, unfair, or just wrong.
- Shame, the feeling that you don't deserve kindness and support, including from yourself.
- A sense of futility, hopelessness, and helplessness; "Why bother since it won't work out anyway?"
- Dismissiveness, indifference, even cruelty toward parts of yourself.

In the pages to come, we'll explore many ways to move through blocks like these. Just being aware of them is very helpful. You can be curious about them while not *identifying* with them. You can recognize where blocks have come from, such as your upbringing, or how other people have treated you. Because we are such social beings, we naturally internalize and do to ourselves what others have done to us, especially during childhood.

You can challenge the beliefs that underpin blocks, with questions like these: *Is this actually true? How often does that really happen? If it's all right for me to be loyal to others, and it's all right for others to be loyal to me, why would it be wrong for me to be loyal to myself?* You can tell yourself what's true, such as: *I couldn't stop that bully in school, but today I am* not *helpless and can stand up for myself . . . What my uncle did was a shame on him, not me; I am* not *broken, tainted, or unworthy of love.*

You can have a sense of disengaging from a block, no longer agreeing with it and reinforcing it, letting it fade, letting it go. Inside your mind, it can be "over there" while the core of you is separated from it. Try telling it that it no longer has power over you; try saying good-bye to it.

Strengthening Loyalty to Yourself

Recall times that you were strong on your own behalf, perhaps once when you had to dig deep to get through a horrible situation or relationship. Try to get a sense, again, of what that strength felt like in order to reinforce it inside yourself. What was the look in your eyes, the expression on your face? Appreciate the ways that you *have* been loyal to yourself, and recognize their benefits, such as helping you to say something important to one of your parents.

In the present, you can be in touch with the sense of being loyal to yourself. Explore it as you experience it, including the feeling of it in your body. Notice things that are meaningful and important for you in being on your own side. Enjoy it! Open to the sense of being for yourself, and let it sink in, all the way in.

You can make a sacred commitment to yourself that you won't let yourself down. That you will keep faith with yourself. Not placing yourself above others, nor placing yourself beneath them. You can respect yourself, and stand by and for and with yourself at each step down the long road of life.

2

Let Be, Let Go, Let In

Stress is normal. Feeling irritated, hurt, or worried is normal. Childhood casts a long shadow, and past losses and wounds naturally affect us today. Life is a bumpy ride, and the world can look pretty scary. Other people can be disappointing, uncaring, or hostile—and sometimes even worse.

Understandably, we have reactions to all these things. And these reactions are shaped and intensified by the brain's negativity bias, which makes it like Velcro for bad experiences but Teflon for good ones.

What can we do?

One option is to do nothing, and just be triggered, hijacked, flooded, or frozen. I've been there—a lot. Sometimes I've been so angry at someone that I lashed out with horrible words, or so hurt that I could hardly move. Besides these intense moments, we can spend much time worrying, rehashing old conversations, or ruminating about resentments. Meanwhile, your mood in general might become chronically anxious, prickly, or blue. It can feel like you're stuck with your mind as it is.

The other option is to *practice* with your thoughts and feelings, desires and actions. This means stepping back from them, rather than being swept away by them, and gradually nudging them in a better direction.

I grew up in a loving and decent home, but I was still very unhappy and twisted up inside by the time I left for college. So I've needed to do a great deal of practice! Over the years, I found help in clinical psychology, contemplative wisdom, and brain science. Just about everything I've learned about practicing with the mind fits into three categories: being with what you're experiencing, reducing what's harmful and painful, and increasing what's helpful and enjoyable. Imagine that your mind is like a garden; you can witness it, pull weeds, and grow flowers. In sum: let be, let go, and let in.

Without practice, we're helpless in the face of the emotional storms inside. With practice, we have *choice*, and a path of healing and happiness. Let's see how to do it.

How

Let Be

First, you can *be with* your experience as it is, both opening to it and observing it, with acceptance and kindness toward whatever you find. It's like watching the movie of your mind from twenty rows back, rather than being stuck to the screen. As you be with it, your experience might shift—for instance, the sense of upset might fade—but you're not trying to influence it directly.

Let's say that someone has criticized you. You could start by recognizing your various reactions, perhaps noting them simply to yourself, such as: *startled . . . annoyed . . . how could they say that—it's unfair! . . . hurt . . . wanting to snap back at them.* Research shows that just labeling the flotsam and jetsam in the stream of consciousness helps to calm down the "alarm bell" in the brain, the amygdala.

You could be aware of different aspects of your experience,

such as sensations of tightening in your belly, or thoughts about why you're right and they're wrong. Underneath surface reactions like anger could be softer feelings, such as sadness, perhaps from deeper parts of yourself that were hurt when you were young. You might understand ways that you're affected by past, even traumatic, events or by current factors, such as financial troubles or ongoing prejudice and bias.

Being able to be with what you're experiencing is the foundation of all other practices. Sometimes, that's all you can do: Perhaps you've experienced a big shock, or every time you think of a loved one you've lost, a deep sense of grief and mourning sweeps through you. And as you heal and grow, more and more you'll simply be resting in a fundamental underlying sense of resilient well-being as various experiences pass through your awareness.

But being with the mind is not the only way to practice. Sometimes we need to *work with it* as well. Painful or harmful thoughts, feelings, habits, and desires are based in neural structures and processes that generally don't change without active efforts to alter them. And anything you'd like to develop inside yourself—from interpersonal skills to general feelings of self-worth, calm, and happiness—will be enhanced by deliberate efforts to produce specific physical changes in your brain.

Just as a bird needs two wings, practicing with your mind requires both *being with* and *working with* in order to fly.

Let Go

Let's say you've been with an experience for a few breaths or minutes or even days, and it feels right to start working with it. Perhaps you're getting flooded by old pain and need to move on from it, at least for now; I've emptied my own bucket of tears a spoonful at a time. Or maybe an all-too-familiar reaction has been triggered, and there's no more value to be had in exploring it.

So you shift into letting go. You're not resisting your thoughts and feelings, but gently *releasing* them.

Using the example of someone criticizing you, you could:

- Deliberately relax that tightening in your belly, breathing into it, softening and easing it.
- Challenge some of your thoughts, perhaps by asking yourself questions like these: *What's just not true about the criticism—so I don't need to worry about that part? . . . Is any part of the criticism true—so I can make use of that part? . . . To the thoughts that say I'm stupid or a failure or unlovable, I say: "You're wrong! In all kinds of ways, I'm actually smart and successful and definitely lovable!"*
- Get a sense of your feelings flowing outward and away. Try venting appropriately (with the intention of releasing, not getting more revved up), such as by writing a letter you won't send or just letting the tears flow for a while. Imagine particular emotions, such as hurt or anger, draining out of you with every exhalation.
- Recognize any desires or plans that are probably not good for you, or for others, such as overreacting in ways you'll regret later. Tell yourself the reasons they're not good.
- Disengage from preoccupations with the past, and focus on the present. Imagine that your hand is holding your reactions like stones, and then open it and let them go.

You don't need to do all these practices! Any one of them might be good, and you'll find your own natural wisdom about what helps to give you a feeling of release, of lightening and clearing in your mind.

Let In

Then you move into focusing on and strengthening what's useful and enjoyable. In the garden of the mind, now you're planting flowers where once were weeds.

For example, if you have been criticized, you could:

- Straighten up a little if you've hunched over a bit to protect yourself.
- Name two or three "wise thoughts" to yourself—such as: *Everybody makes mistakes, and it's not the end of the world . . . Every day, I do many things correctly and effectively . . . I have really good intentions!*—and repeat them, and help yourself *believe* them.
- Gently invite positive feelings, particularly ones that are a kind of antidote to how the criticism made you feel. Since criticism can feel belittling and rejecting, try to recall the feeling of being with people who appreciate you and make you feel valued.
- Identify any intentions or plans that you want to support in the days to come. Perhaps there's a good lesson to learn from the criticism—which might include taking a step back from people who don't treat you well.

As you experience what you're letting in, stay with it for a breath or longer, getting a sense of it in your body, and being aware of what's enjoyable or meaningful about it. Doing this will help that experience leave lasting traces behind in your brain.

Without those changes in your nervous system, the experience in the moment might have felt good, but afterward there was no *learning* from it, no healing, no greater skillfulness, resilience, or happiness. Besides experiencing it, you can *grow* from it, too.

And if you know that it would help you to develop particular *inner resources*, such as more confidence around other people, you can look for ways to experience that resource and then help it sink deeply into you, becoming a part of you that's with you wherever you go. (For more about the practical neuroscience of "taking in the good," please see my book, *Hardwiring Happiness*.)

In the Garden of the Mind

When something is stressful or painful, there is a natural rhythm that often flows from letting be to letting go and then to letting in. But if it's especially upsetting, such as stirring up an old trauma, it could be useful to start by focusing on—letting in—the sense of calm strength or feeling loved by someone, which will help you be with the experience when that feels right. You could imagine that people you care about are with you as you face your pain, and they're being compassionate, supportive, and encouraging.

As you practice with your mind, you'll learn many interesting and useful things about yourself. You'll become more relaxed and effective with others, better able to stay centered during conflicts and recover from upsets. It will be easier to keep your heart open, even when you need to stand up for yourself. You won't be so affected by things that have happened in the past. You'll be better able to deal with the unavoidable stresses and injustices of our very imperfect world. Knowing what it's like to take responsibility for your own mind and to practice with it, you'll be in a better position—when it's appropriate—to ask others to do the same.

Practice is usually a matter of small steps over time. So it's completely doable, even in very tough circumstances. In fact, the worse that a person's life is, the more valuable it is to practice. Even when the outer world is stuck in a really bad place, you can always heal and grow a little each day inside yourself. Breath by breath, synapse by synapse, you can gradually develop a resilient well-being that's hardwired into your nervous system.

3

Rest in Calm Strength

When I look back on forty years of marriage, raising two kids, and many kinds of relationships with friends, family, coworkers, and others, it's clear that most of my painful experiences and most of my interpersonal mistakes happened when I was feeling stressed and rattled.

How about you? Would you say much the same thing?

We get stressed and rattled when it feels like an important need is not being met. Grounded in our biology, each of us has a fundamental need to be *safe*, *satisfied*, and *connected* (broadly speaking). When it feels like these needs are being met, the body naturally settles down and repairs and refuels itself. In the mind, there's often a related sense of calming, thankfulness, and kindness, perhaps in the background of awareness. This is our healthy resting state, which I call the Green Zone. Centered in it, you can *be with* physical or emotional pain without being invaded or overwhelmed by it. You can handle relationship issues from a place of self-confidence and compassion—even when you have to be assertive.

But when you feel that an important need is not being met, your body kicks into its stress response of fighting, fleeing, or freezing. Meanwhile, depending on the need in question, in your mind there could be a sense of:

- Fear, anger, or helplessness (when you don't feel physically or emotionally safe).

- Frustration, disappointment, boredom, drivenness, or addiction (when satisfaction feels out of reach).
- Hurt, shame, inadequacy, envy, resentment, or hostility (when you don't feel connected with others in positive ways).

This is the Red Zone. Sometimes it's subtle, such as being preoccupied with a hurtful interaction with someone at work. Other times it's intense, like in the middle of a fight with a partner. Repeated Red Zone experiences, even seemingly mild ones, wear down your physical and mental health. For example, a US surgeon general, Dr. Vivek Murthy, has pointed out that chronic loneliness shortens the average life span about as much as smoking a half-pack of cigarettes a day.

How

To spend more time in the Green Zone and less in the Red, the prescription is simple:

1. Develop and use psychological resources, such as grit, self-worth, and interpersonal skills, to meet your needs more effectively, and without having to go Red to do it.
2. When it feels like a need is being sufficiently met *in the present*—for instance, maybe a relationship isn't perfect, but still you feel pretty connected and cared about—slow down to take this experience into yourself. Bit by bit, you'll be growing an underlying sense of peacefulness, contentment, and love.

This book is all about #1, developing and using psychological resources in your relationships, with occasional reminders to do

#2 as well. It's also certainly helpful to improve conditions out in the world and inside your body. But those can be slow to change. Meanwhile, you can quickly build up the attitudes and capabilities that foster better relationships—starting with a foundation of calm strength.

Come to Center

In some ways other people are like the wind—sometimes warm and gentle, other times cold and stormy. So it helps to have a sense of deep roots, like a strong tree. Then you can withstand the strongest winds without being knocked over. In your body, the *parasympathetic nervous system* (PNS) promotes this feeling of being calm and centered. Try taking a couple of breaths with l-o-n-g exhalations, and notice how that feels. You're experiencing the PNS, since it is involved with exhaling and slowing the heart rate. You could scan your body and systematically release tension in different parts of it—also engaging the PNS. With repetition, studies show that this *relaxation response* will become a kind of (very good) habit, and even change the expression of genes in your brain to make you more resilient.

If you're starting to tip into the Red Zone, take some of those long exhalations and increase parasympathetic activation to dial down the *sympathetic nervous system* (SNS), which revs up when we feel stressed. These two branches of the autonomic nervous system are connected like a seesaw: When one goes up, it pushes the other one down.

As you breathe, tune into the internal sensations of air flowing in and out, and your lungs expanding and contracting. This will help you feel grounded in your own body and stable inside—even when the breezes from other people really begin to blow.

Notice You're Alright Right Now

Much of the information entering your brain comes from inside your body. Unless you're experiencing great physical or emotional pain, those signals are like the calls of a night watchman: "All is well, all is well." There *is* enough air to breathe, your heart *is* beating, your organs *are* working, your mind *is* functioning, your awareness *is* ongoing. Things may be far from perfect, but you're basically OK. Whatever the past has been and the future may be, you're basically alright *right now*.

It's extremely useful to notice this!

It's reassuring and calming, an immediate antidote to anxiety. When it's true—and it usually is—you can find your footing in a sense of basic alrightness *in the present*. Around the edges may well be pain and sorrow, real issues to deal with. But in the center of your being, you're OK. Recognizing this and really feeling it doesn't mean ignoring threats or getting complacent. It actually makes you stronger if you have to take action against those who harm you or others.

Try it: Over the course of a breath, keep noticing the *fact* that you're basically OK, and help yourself feel some reassurance, and an easing of uneasiness or tension. If your mind wanders to the past or the future, that's normal; just return to the present, noticing that you're alright now, and now, and now.

Know That You're Strong

Many people don't appreciate how strong they really are. Strong in their determination, clarity of purpose, and heart. You don't need to look like a bodybuilder to have grit, patience, and endurance.

Take a moment to tune into a sense of strength inside. You could feel the natural vitality in breathing, in the ongoing livingness of your own body. Recall a time when you felt strong, perhaps out in the wilderness, working with tools, or holding a pose in yoga. Remember a time when you were knocked sideways by something but then you found your footing; in this recovery is real strength. Get a sense of these experiences in your body today, and be aware of what feels good about them.

If you like, stay in touch with feeling strong while bringing to mind a difficult relationship. Imagine the other person speaking forcefully, maybe criticizing you or telling you what to do, while you simply keep feeling strong, deep down inside. Keep returning to and reinforcing that sense of strength. You might feel nervous or unsure or sad—while also having a deeply rooted sense of your own strength. Just this—simply feeling strong while being challenged—will help you stay calm and centered when the world is flashing Red.

4

Feel Cared About

We all know what it feels like to care about others—perhaps a friend, a partner, or a pet. There's a sense of warm connection, that something good is flowing from you to them.

It's equally important to feel cared about *yourself*. To feel that you are included, seen, appreciated, liked, or loved.

Wanting to feel cared about can be a little . . . embarrassing. But it's a totally normal desire, and one that's grounded in our biology as very social beings. Starting 200 million years ago with the first mammals, our ancestors evolved in large part by getting better at caring for each other. Our own species has been here for around 300,000 years, most of that time in small hunter-gatherer bands of forty to fifty people; exile from that group could be a death sentence, and mattering to others was crucial to basic survival. Those who didn't care about feeling cared about were less likely to pass on their genes. No wonder we want others to care about us!

Today, being understood, valued, and cherished may not be a life-or-death matter. But studies do show that feeling cared about lowers stress, increases positive emotions, encourages ambition, and promotes resilience. Unfortunately, many of us have experienced abandonment, rejection, shaming, or abuse—often in childhood when we're particularly vulnerable. Even if past experiences didn't leave a *wound*—the presence of the bad—there's frequently a significant *lack*, something important missing: the absence of the good. We all need to feel wanted, recognized, and nurtured. *Social supplies* like these feed the emotional heart just as good food nourishes the body. For example, I was not bullied or abused, but because I was shy and very young in school, and my parents were busy, the social supplies coming to me were like a thin soup, and I ended up feeling as if there were a big empty hole in my heart.

Both to ease old pain and to get through everyday life, it's important to feel cared about. For me, it's been a crucial part of my own healing. No matter what your past has been and no matter how hard and isolated your life is today, you can always find ways to feel genuinely cared about, and to gradually fill up any hole in your own heart.

How

Let's start with the hard part: Opening to feeling cared about can bring up past experiences of *not* feeling so cared about. Perhaps you've had a disengaged or critical parent—or partner. Seemingly small moments of being left out, let down, or put down often leave painful traces behind. Try to let these feelings be, accepting them and holding them in a large space of awareness so they are not so overwhelming.

Then, take a breath, and turn to the other side of the truth: the ways and times that you *have* been cared about in the past and *are* cared about today. Those really exist! They do in everyone's life. There is a range of caring—from mild to intense, and from being included, seen, or appreciated to being liked and even loved. It may not be perfect or sustained, so it might be tempting to think it's not good enough. But it's still a genuine nutrient for a hungry heart.

Building Up an Emotional Memory Bank

So look for the *facts* of caring for you throughout your day. Most of these will be brief moments when someone is sincerely thoughtful, friendly, or concerned. Small as they may be, they are real, and you can help the recognition of them become a *feeling* of being cared about. Try to slow down and stay with the experience: What's it like to feel included? To feel seen or appreciated? What's the sense in your body of being cared about? How does it feel to be liked? To be loved?

Doing this might stir up fears of disappointment, even betrayal, based on your personal history. It's poignant and sad: We long to feel cared about but, to avoid being hurt again, we may push the feeling away. If you have these normal doubts and fears, look again at the *fact* of the caring truly coming your way.

Try to recognize ongoing sources of caring for you. For example, bring to mind a group that feels good to be part of, or someone who respects you at work, or compassionate friends and family members, or a favorite pet. They do feel grateful to you, they do like you, they do wish you well. Can you take a breath or two and open to feeling this?

You can also recall caring that's come to you in the past. Perhaps a grandparent making cookies, teammates and teachers, parents and mentors, people who saw good in you and opened doors and blessed you on your way. Some of these people may no longer be in your life, and you might also feel some sadness. Nonetheless, when you bring to mind the fact of their caring for you in the past, you can feel cared about again in the present.

Know what it feels like to be cared about. Stay with the experience, open to it in your body, and notice what feels good about it. You can let these warm good feelings soothe old hurts like a healing balm, even giving deeper layers of yourself some of what was missing when you were young. Before you fall asleep, call to mind the sense of being cared about, and rest in that feeling as it weaves its way into your breathing, body, and dreams. In effect, you're making deposits in an emotional memory bank. Then, when life is challenging and others are clueless or cold, you can tune into the sense that you *have* been cared about and that you *are* cared about—no matter what else is happening.

Your Caring Committee

It's normal to have different sub-personalities, perspectives, "voices," or "energies" inside yourself, and we'll explore this idea further in the next chapter. For example, there's a part of me that sets the alarm clock early to get up and exercise, and then there's another part of me the next morning that says, *Nah, not today. Back to sleep.*

Some parts tear us down—*That was a huge mistake. You keep messing up. No one's going to really love you*—while other parts build us up with realistic guidance, compassion, and kindness. Some parts can join together to form a kind of inner attacker while other parts form an inner supporter. Unfortunately, for many people the inner attacker is like giant Godzilla but the inner supporter is like little Bambi.

It's helpful to recognize the inner attacker for what it is: well-intended, maybe, but way over the top. Try to step back from it and don't identify with it. See if it has anything useful to say, and then shift your attention elsewhere. Rather than arguing with it, like some annoying troll online, focus on building up your inner supporter.

A great way to do this is to develop a kind of *caring committee* inside that helps you in a variety of ways. My own committee includes an internalized feeling of people who've loved me, good buddies, tough-but-kind coaches, and spiritual teachers. I've got a goofy imagination, so there's also a sense of Obi-Wan Kenobi, Gandalf, and the fairy godmothers from Sleeping Beauty. When you're with people who are caring in some way—perhaps really listening to you, giving you good advice, or cheering you on—slow down to receive that experience into yourself and gradually strengthen the neural basis of your inner supporter. You could even make a little list or drawing of who's on your own caring committee.

Tune into these supportive parts of yourself whenever you feel hurt or lonely. Imagine listening to them and getting emotional support and wise counsel as if you had a good friend inside. You can imagine that the caring committee is sticking up for you against the inner attacker; as a powerful exercise, you could write out a dialogue between them. You can feel that your caring committee is protective and nurturing toward the parts inside you—we all have them—that are young, soft, or vulnerable.

As you strengthen the sense of being cared about in these various ways, you will naturally become more caring toward others. Remarkably, it's good for them for *you* to feel cared about.

5

Accept Yourself

If you've ever spent time with an infant or toddler, you can see yourself as you were many years ago. We are born whole, with everything included—the full range of emotions and desires. It's like being a great mansion with all the doors open to all the rooms.

Then life happens. So many situations and people, pleasures and pains . . . and gradually doors may close, locking up what's inside. By fifteen months (the age of the toddlers studied in my PhD dissertation), you can see clear differences in these little people. Some are still open and well-integrated psychologically. Yet others are already pushing down certain feelings and becoming internally divided—which is what happened for me. My earliest memories, from about age two onward, are tinged with caution around other people. As the years passed, I lost touch with many feelings, especially the softer, more vulnerable ones. I longed to be close to others, but was afraid of what they might see if I lowered my guard.

If you suppress or disown parts of yourself, feeling bad about who you are can easily follow, with the sense that there are nasty, weak, shameful, or unlovable things inside you. It may feel uneasy and tense to keep so much at bay. We end up playing small around others to keep them away from all that we cannot accept about ourselves.

How

Sure, some of the rooms in the mansion of the mind contain intensities and impulses that need to be regulated. But at least we can put a window in those doors and know what is behind them. You can be wise and appropriate about what you reveal about yourself to others while still being fully revealed to *yourself*; this fosters greater confidence and self-worth. You can become more comfortable with just being yourself with others—more open, more vulnerable, more *real*—without needing to put up a social front or muzzle yourself or worry about their judgments and approval.

Accept Your Experiences

In chapter 2, we explored simply *being with* what is passing through your awareness. With this stance toward your own mind, you can open to all five major aspects of our experiences:

- Thoughts—beliefs, interpretations, perspectives, images, memories
- Perceptions—sensations, sights, sounds, tastes, smells
- Emotions—feelings, attitudes
- Desires—wishes, wants, needs, longings, dreams, values, intentions, plans
- Actions—postures, facial expressions, gestures, behaviors

Ask yourself: *How in touch am I with every aspect of my experiences in the list above? Are there certain experiences that I ignore, push away, fear, or deny—such as anger or certain memories from childhood?* Personally, it felt like I entered adulthood numb from the neck down. I was aware of my thoughts but the rest of my inner world was like a forbidden land, and I had to gradually reclaim it. Again and again, slowly but surely, it helped to do simple practices like the one below. I encourage you to try it:

1. Any time you like—both when you're relaxed and when something (or someone!) is bothering you—slow down a bit, take a few breaths, and establish a basic sense of calm strength and feeling cared about.

2. Ask yourself: What am I experiencing now? Step back and observe your thoughts . . . sensations throughout your body . . . emotions, both soft ones like sadness and hard ones like anger . . . desires, from gentle longings to fierce cravings . . . and actions, embodied in posture, facial expressions, and movements. Stay in the present and rest in the witnessing of what you're experiencing, in touch with it without being carried away by it.

3. Be aware of resisting anything, getting tense about it, or pushing it away—and see if you can let go of doing that. Try to soften and open around what is present in awareness, letting it flow as it will. Keep opening to what might be deeper, younger, more charged and upsetting, more vulnerable.

If anything feels overwhelming, step back from it, reestablish a sense of openhearted calm strength, and then see if you can return to awareness of it. It's OK to keep moving from one aspect of your experience to another. It may help to label things briefly to yourself, such as: *feeling hurt . . . tension in my belly . . . resentment . . . thoughts of revenge . . . feeling let down by others . . . memories of childhood . . .*

Try to accept what you're experiencing as it is, without making

it good or bad, right or wrong. It might be painful, it might be pleasurable; in any case, it's here, it's a human experience, it's occurring due to various causes and conditions, many of which extend beyond you to other people, other times, and other places. You could softly say to yourself: *I accept that I feel _____.*
I accept that I want _____. I accept that thoughts of
_____ *are arising.* As the psychologist and mindfulness teacher Tara Brach puts it, you could say to yourself: *This, too, belongs.*

Notice what it feels like to be accepting toward your experiences. Be aware of any greater sense of ease, centeredness, wholeness, or peacefulness. Appreciate yourself for having the courage and strength to be open to all that can arise in awareness.

Accept the Parts of Yourself

Your brain is one of the most complex physical objects known to science. Inside your head are about 85 billion neurons amid another 100 billion support cells, organized in different regions—such as the prefrontal cortex, the amygdala, and the tegmentum—to accomplish different functions. A typical neuron makes several thousand connections with other neurons, giving you a vast network of several hundred trillion synapses, each one like a little microprocessor. No wonder the neuroscientist Charles Sherrington called the brain an "enchanted loom," continuously weaving the tapestry of consciousness.

Since your brain has many parts, *you* have many parts as well. Some may be tight and anxious; others might be looser and braver. Some like order, others long for wildness. Some parts are chatty, while others communicate with images and feelings. Some feel adult, and some feel young. Some want to eat/drink/smoke a particular molecule, or yammer away critically, or hold on to resentments toward others. Other parts offer a deep inner wisdom. Some parts want to get closer to other people, while different parts may want to pull away.

Parts that have been praised and rewarded push forward, and they're what we typically present to the world. Parts that got us into trouble as children usually withdraw to the shadows, perhaps with a feeling of shame . . . or maybe a growing fury. When we overreact to others, it's often because we've seen something in them that we've scorned and exiled in *ourselves.*

This inner complexity has been long recognized, from Shakespeare ("to be or not to be") and Freud ("id, ego, superego") to Richard Schwartz's theory of "internal family systems." As the poet Walt Whitman put it, "I contain multitudes." This is *normal*— and recognizing that it's not a problem with you personally is a big step toward accepting yourself more fully. (Extremes of inner conflict, fragmentation of the self, and what's known as dissociative identity disorder call for professional help that's beyond the scope of this book.) Each part of you is trying to help you, even if in misguided ways. You can expand your sense of self to include *all* of you, which releases the tension of inner conflict, makes use of the gifts of each part, eases your relationships with others, and brings a peaceful sense of inner wholeness. Let's explore this in three experiential ways.

In a written list, a drawing, or your imagination, identify some of your many parts.

Give each part a name with a word or phrase. For example, I could label some of my parts as follows: rebellious child, controlling parent, woodsman, monk, dogged worker, angry warrior, playful goofball, sad witness of the world, encourager, and wounded withdrawer. You can be creative with this, and imagine your inner tree of wisdom, Athena, snake, trickster, or rock star. Try to recognize beautiful, important, valuable parts of yourself—qualities, intentions, inclinations, intuitions, abilities—that you may have set aside, pushed down, or denied. Acknowledge parts of yourself that you'd like to offer more to others. Whatever it is, it's all you!

Next, imagine that these parts of you are all sitting quietly in a circle, perhaps at a large round table. Get a sense of the core of yourself, a center of awareness, good-heartedness, wisdom, and decision: the essence of your "I." Then from this center, recognize each of your parts and in your mind say something like this: *[Name of this part], I recognize you. You're a part of me. You're trying to help me in your way. I include you. I accept you. Thank you.* Be aware of your reactions to various parts of yourself, particularly ones that you've pushed away. Try to accept each part of you for what it is. Accept that the whole of you does indeed include this part, even if you need to regulate it. Remember that you can accept a part of yourself without being hijacked by it.

Explore dialogues with some of your parts.

A simple way to do this is to imagine that the core of you is talking with a part: not trying to persuade or change it, but rather just hearing it out. Here's a brief sample dialogue with a free-spirited child part:

CORE "I": Hello, free-spirited child. I would really like to talk with you. Will you talk with me?
FREE-SPIRITED CHILD: OK! But don't be boring!
CORE: OK, I'll try not to be boring. Do you like to play?

CHILD: Yes!

CORE: What do you especially like to do?

CHILD: I like it when we run around and have fun and not work all the time.

CORE: Do you feel sad or mad that I work a lot?

CHILD: Yes. Both!

CORE: Thank you for telling me. Do you have anything else to say?

CHILD: Nah, not now. This is getting boring.

CORE: OK, we can stop now. Thanks for talking with me.

Remember that the core of you doesn't have to agree with any part or do what it says. You can keep reestablishing a sense of calm strength. Try to be open to the attitudes and desires of the different parts of yourself. Interestingly, the more you give voice to your parts, the more they'll tend to settle down and become connected and balanced with each other.

You can apply this notion of parts of yourself to a particular conflict or to a generally challenging relationship.

Suppose you just had an argument after your partner criticized you. You could take some minutes to ask yourself questions like these—with some possible answers in brackets:

What parts of me have gotten stirred up by this? [Feeling Hurt part; Angry part; Wanting to Feel Loved part]

OK, let's listen to each of these parts. What do you have to say? [Feeling Hurt part: I'm really sad. Angry part: This isn't fair, let's get out of here! Wanting to Feel Loved part: I just want to feel cared about, and not hurt and pushed away.]

Is there a part I need to listen to more? And express more in this relationship? [the Wanting to Feel Loved part]

And is there a part that I need to be mindful of and not let it hijack me? [yep, the Angry part]

Hmm. Now that I've made room for each of these parts, how do I feel? [probably calmer and more integrated]

Taking them all into account, what should I do? What's the best path from here? [tell my partner that I do want to hear what they want, but without all their angry tone and accusations]

With practices like these, you will feel less yanked this way and that by competing "voices" and reactions inside yourself. This will help you be more open and authentic around others. You'll feel less identified with and swept along by any particular part of yourself, with a greater sense of yourself as a *whole*.

6

Respect Your Needs

We live *dependently*, needing many many things for physical survival, happiness, love, and all that we want to accomplish. Second by second, our lives depend on oxygen, the plants that "exhale" it, the sun that drives photosynthesis, and the other stars that exploded billions of years ago to make every atom of oxygen in the next breath we take. From the moment of conception, we also need other people. You and I and everyone else are frail, soft, vulnerable, hurt by little things, and hungry for love. When we accept this universal fact, we're not so hard on ourselves—and others.

Many people feel needy or ashamed about their needs and deep wants. (I won't try to split hairs between what is a *need* and what is a *deep want*, and will use both terms synonymously.) But needs are normal; we all have them. Simply recognizing this can feel calming and ease self-criticism. The first step in getting others to meet your needs better is to respect your needs *yourself*.

How

In your mind, out loud, on paper, or with a trusted friend, try a little experiment in which you start a sentence with: *I need* _____ , and fill in the blank. Then do it again and again. Just say what comes to mind, even if it seems silly. As you repeatedly complete the sentence, you may find that you're getting deeper, into more fundamental needs. When it feels like you've expressed what there is to say, at least for now, try different sentence stems such as: *I really want* _____ . . . *It's important to me to feel* _____ . . . *When I get what I need,* _____ . Next, try this exercise again while focusing on one or more specific relationships.

Then, pick one of your needs, and say to yourself things like this: *I do need* _____ . . . *I accept that I really value* _____ . . . _____ *is very important to me . . . It's normal and OK that I need* _____ . Try to soften inside and help yourself feel OK about having this need.

Take another step and ask yourself if there is a deeper need under this one. For example, you might have come up with "I need more compliments from my spouse." But compliments are a means to the end of a deeper need, such as needing to have a sense of self-worth. We can get caught up in trying to satisfy superficial, means-to-an-end needs, sometimes by becoming fixated on particular words or behaviors from others. One reason for this is that it may feel safer to talk about these "proxies" for deep vulnerable needs. For instance, when our kids were young, I asked my wife if she could give me a hug when I got home from work. Sure, affection was nice, but what I really needed was to feel that I still mattered to her as a being, not just as a co-parent—and that was a lot scarier to say out loud. Even if you can get someone to say the "right" things, your deeper need may not feel fulfilled if *it* is not directly addressed.

Once you identify a down-deep need, consider what you could do to honor it more fully. (You can repeat this process for other needs, too). It might seem that the deeper the need, the harder it is to meet it. But actually, our deepest needs are usually about having an important *experience*, such as feeling peaceful, contented, or loved. When you shift your focus from reality having to be a certain way—such as from getting a compliment or a hug—to what you need to *feel* inside, then there are usually lots of ways to help yourself have that experience. This is wonderfully freeing! Ask yourself: *What would I feel deep down if others did what I wanted them to do or say?* And then ask yourself this crucial question: *How could I help myself have that experience without being so bound to what other people do?*

For example, if you want a greater sense of self-worth, you could look for ways that other people do appreciate and value you, without them saying a word. You could recognize some of the many things you accomplish in a day, and really take in the feeling of your capabilities. Before you get out of bed in the morning and before you go to sleep at night, you could tune into your fundamental kindness and caring for others. All of these are entirely within your own power. There's certainly a place for speaking skillfully with others—including about their needs, too—and for some suggestions about how to do this, please see the chapters in parts four and five. But it's all too easy to get stuck in a sense of unmet needs because other people just won't, you know, act the right way! Then you might feel helpless, even despairing. It's really good to make a plan for how *you* will respect your needs more fully—especially if you've been raised or treated in ways that criticized or downplayed your needs. Instead of waiting for others to meet them, it's empowering, hopeful, and healing to take responsibility yourself for doing all that you can to experience that your deep needs are being sufficiently met. While we do depend on other people, we can take responsibility within that field of dependence, which over time will probably help you be more effective when it's time to ask for things from others.

Last, consider how you also depend on . . . *you*. The you that you are today has been gifted in thousands of ways, large and small, by previous versions of yourself. Like runners in a great relay race, you hand the baton each day to the you who wakes up the next morning. No matter what mistakes you've made in the past, think of some of the many things that earlier you's have contributed to your life: problems solved, goals accomplished, dishes done, relationships nurtured, lessons learned. What would it feel like to imagine some of those previous you's, and thank them?

Looking forward, consider how your future you depends on what you do today. Not as pressure, but gently, let it sink in that your future you is counting on you, right now. What will be important to this being that you will become? What could you do this year, this day, that would set up this future person to live with safety, health, happiness, and ease?

7

Have Compassion for Yourself

Think about a friend or even a stranger who is suffering. They could be weary from a long day of work or worried about their children. They could be dealing with a chronic illness, stressed about money, or feeling lonely while longing for a partner.

If you knew about their pain, you'd probably feel some compassion for them. You'd have empathy for what they're going through, warmhearted concern and caring, and the desire to help if you could.

But when you're the one who is suffering, how often do you have compassion for yourself? Most people find it a lot easier to be sympathetic and supportive toward others than toward themselves.

Yet much research shows that self-compassion has many benefits. Beginning with the groundbreaking work of professor Kristin Neff, studies have found that it makes people more resilient, confident, and ambitious. It lowers stress, reduces harsh self-criticism, and boosts self-worth. In a challenging relationship, self-compassion will ease the impacts of others on you, soften your anger, and help you interact in a more self-respecting and heartfelt way. It's *not* wallowing in self-pity; it makes you stronger, not weaker. When you're knocked sideways by life, start by having some compassion for yourself; then you can figure out what to do next.

How

Suffering is a broad term that covers both physical and mental pain, from subtle to intense. It is not the whole of life, but it's certainly part of it for everyone—and, unfortunately, a very large part for many people. Mental suffering includes experiences of sadness, fear, hurt, and anger, as well as stress, pressure, numbing, loneliness, frustration, disappointment, guilt, shame, negative rumination, self-criticism, and basically any sense that something's missing or wrong. Life lands on everyone; we all carry burdens; we all lose loved ones; we all face illness, aging, and death.

Can you take a moment to tune into your own suffering? It might just be a background feeling of fatigue, uneasiness about getting everything done today, or soft heartache about a particular relationship. Whatever it is, it's there and it's real.

Our suffering is the result of numerous things, both inside and outside us. Regardless of its source, pain is pain, no matter what the cause, and you can bring compassion to it. You can have compassion for yourself, even if you feel you're responsible for some of your suffering.

Once you acknowledge your suffering—allowing it, not pushing it away—you can bring a sense of caring and support to it. Compassion is bittersweet: There is both the bitter of the suffering and the sweet of the good wishes and tender concern. While staying aware of the bitter, focus mainly on the sweet. If your attention gets pulled into the pain or if it wanders into criticizing yourself or others, just bring it back—if need be, again and again—to a feeling of caring and support.

When we feel compassion, there is a natural movement toward doing what we can to relieve the suffering. Yet sometimes there is nothing we can do. Your compassion is still genuine, and it matters in its own right, even when there's nothing you can "fix." Even if you're dealing with intractable situations—perhaps a sibling who won't talk to you or a stressful job to keep your health insurance—you can still bring warmth and respect to yourself about them.

Let's say you've been feeling strained, even upset, in a challenging relationship. Try this extended practice of self-compassion:

Start by getting in touch with the sense of being calm and strong . . . and feeling cared about. Next, bring to mind someone you care about . . . recognize some of their suffering . . . find compassion for them . . . and know what it's like to be compassionate.

Then be aware of what you're experiencing in this challenging relationship. Mainly focus on your emotions and sensations and longings, and try to disengage from rehashing past events. You could softly name the aspects of your suffering, such as: *sad . . . annoyed . . . kind of stunned . . . so tired . . . worried . . . a weight in the pit of my stomach . . . feel like a kid sent to the principal's office . . . throat's tight . . . memories from high school of being pushed out of a group . . . mind whirling with what I should have said . . . why doesn't anyone stick up for me?! . . . very angry . . . hurt, actually, really hurt . . .*

While you're acknowledging what you're feeling, find some understanding and warmth for yourself, just as you would for a friend who was feeling much the same. You might imagine yourself sitting in a chair in front of you, or have a sense of places that are hurting inside you. In whatever ways that feel right to you, your caring, tender concern and support are flowing toward the suffering. In your mind, you might softly say things like this: *Yes, this is hard . . . yes, this hurts . . . it's OK to feel this; other people feel this, too . . . may I not suffer . . . may this ease . . . may I be at peace . . .* You can recognize our "common humanity," that we suffer because we're human, that you're not alone, that around the world right now many people are feeling something similar to what you are.

It might feel as if warmth and goodwill were rippling out from you in waves toward the suffering. Imagine or sense that compassion is making contact with the suffering, perhaps sinking down into hurting places inside or communicating with younger parts of you. You could put a hand on your heart or your cheek, or give yourself a hug, to deepen the feeling of all this.

Then make a little shift and explore the sense of *receiving* compassion into yourself. What's it like to have been given compassion? Can you let it into yourself? In some ways, can you feel seen, understood, and supported—even if only by yourself?

As you finish a practice of self-compassion, you could see if there are any intuitions or intentions about skillful actions you could take for this challenging relationship—in your mind, with your words, or in your behaviors. You could imagine yourself taking these actions, and experiencing their benefits, and being motivated to take these steps for your own sake and that of others.

8

Know You're a Good Person

For many of us, it's hard to believe that: *I am a basically good person.* You can work hard, learn things, and help others—but feel deeply convinced that you are truly good? Nah!

We end up *not* feeling like a good person in a variety of ways. You might have received a good deal of fault-finding, shaming, moralistic chastising, and other criticisms during childhood—and perhaps more of this as an adult. You could have had experiences of worthlessness, inadequacy, and unlovableness, perhaps also with feelings of guilt and remorse. Almost everyone—including myself—has done some bad things, or said them or thought them. Things like hitting an animal, risking the lives of their children while driving buzzed, being mean to a vulnerable person, stealing from a store, or cheating on a partner. These don't need to be felony offenses to make someone feel that they're not a good person.

Sure, there is a place for healthy remorse. But shining through our lapses of integrity is an underlying and pervading goodness. Deep down, almost all intentions are positive, even if they're expressed in problematic ways. When we are not disturbed by pain or loss or fear, the human brain defaults to a basic equilibrium of calm, contentment, and caring. And in ways that may feel mysterious and profound, you can sense an inherent—and perhaps transpersonal—lovingness and benevolence in the core of your being.

Really, the truth, the *fact*, is that you are a basically good person!

When you feel your own natural goodness, you are more likely to act in good ways. Knowing your own goodness, you're better able to recognize it in others. Seeing the good in yourself and others, you're more likely to do what you can to build the good in the world we share together.

How

I've learned five effective ways to feel like a good person—and feel free to add more.

1. **Take in the good of feeling cared about**—When you have a chance to feel included, seen, appreciated, liked, or loved, stay with this experience for a breath or longer, letting it fill your mind and body, sinking into it as it sinks into you.

2. **Recognize goodness in your thoughts, words, and deeds**—For example, recognize your positive intentions, even if you don't always succeed with them. Notice it when you put the brakes on anger, restrain addictive impulses, or extend compassion and helpfulness to others. Try to appreciate your grit and determination, kindness, courage, generosity, patience, and willingness to see the truth, whatever it is. You are recognizing *facts* about yourself. Create a kind of sanctuary in your mind for this recognition, and protect it from people who make themselves feel big by making others feel small.

3. **Sense the goodness in the core of your being**—It's there inside everyone, even if it's sometimes hard to sense or see. It can feel intimate, and perhaps sacred. A force, a current, a wellspring in your heart.

4. **See the goodness in others**—Recognizing their goodness will help you feel your own. You can observe everyday small acts of fairness, kindness, and honorable effort in others. Sense the deeper layers behind their eyes, the inner longings to be decent and loving, to contribute, to help rather than harm.

5. **Give over to goodness**—Increasingly, let the "better angels of your nature" be the animating force of your life. You could write a little letter in which you tell yourself, most sincerely, why you are a basically good person; from time to time, read it again—and believe it. In tricky situations or relationships, ask yourself, *As a good person, what's appropriate here?* As you act from this goodness, let the knowledge that you are a good person sink in ever more deeply.

Enjoy this beautiful goodness, so real and so true.

9

Trust Yourself

As I grew up, at home and at school it felt dangerous to be myself—my whole self, including the parts that made mistakes, got rebellious and angry, goofed around too loudly, or were awkward and vulnerable. I didn't fear violence, as many have faced, but felt the risk of being punished in other ways, or rejected, shunned, and shamed.

So, as children do, I put on a mask. Closed up, watching warily, managing the performance of "me." There was a valve in my throat: I knew what I thought and felt deep inside, but little of it came out into the world.

From the outside, it looked like I didn't trust other people. Yes, I did need to be careful around some of them. But, mainly, I didn't trust *myself*.

I didn't trust that the authentic me was good enough, lovable enough—and that I'd still be OK if I did mess up. Didn't have confidence in my own depths, that they already contained goodness, wisdom, and love. Didn't trust the unfolding process of living without tight, top-down control. Doubted myself, my worth, my possibilities.

And so I lived all squeezed up, doing well in school and happy sometimes—but mainly swinging between numbness and pain.

In Erik Erikson's eight stages of human development, the first, foundational one is about "basic trust." He focused on trust/mistrust of the outer world (especially the people in it), and, to be sure, this is important. Yet often what seems like *The world is untrustworthy* is, at its root, *I don't trust myself to deal with it.*

It's been a lifelong journey to develop more faith in myself, to lighten up, loosen up, swing out, take chances, make mistakes and then repair and learn from them, and stop taking myself so seriously.

Sure, things might go wrong sometimes when you trust yourself more. But they can go *really* wrong and stay wrong when you trust yourself less.

How

Nobody is perfect. You don't need to be perfect to relax, say what you really feel, and take your full shot at life. It's the big picture that matters most, and the long view. Yes, top-down tight control and a well-crafted persona may bring short-term benefits. But over the long term, the costs are much greater, including stress, bottled-up truths, and inner alienation.

With gentleness and self-compassion, take a look at yourself. Do you doubt yourself and hold back out of fear of looking bad or failing—including in key relationships? If you imagine being your full self out loud, is there an expectation of rejection, misunderstanding, or a shaming attack?

Maybe you've internalized the criticism of others, and have been focusing on what you think is wrong about you.

And missing so much that is already right.

When you ease up and simply let yourself be your natural self, what's that like? How do others respond? When you trust yourself, what are you able to accomplish, at home or at work?

Sure, be prudent about the outer world and recognize when it's truly unwise to let go, take risks, speak out. And guide your inner world like a loving parent, recognizing that not every thought or feeling or want should be voiced or enacted.

Meanwhile, if you are like me and every single person I have ever known who has decided to trust their own deep self, you will find so much that's right inside: so much knowing of what's true and what matters, so much life and heart, so many gifts waiting to be given, so many strengths. Think about an important, perhaps challenging relationship, and consider how it could go better if your trusted yourself more deeply.

Be your whole self; it's your whole self that you can trust. This day, this week, this life—see what happens when you bet on yourself, when you back your own play. See what happens when you let yourself fall backward into your own arms, trusting that they will catch you.

10

Gift Yourself

Can you remember a time when you offered a gift to someone? Perhaps a holiday present, or a treat to a child, or helping out a friend. How did this feel? Researchers have found that giving stimulates some of the same neural networks that light up when we feel physical pleasure.

There is also *receiving*. Can you remember a time when someone was giving toward you? Maybe it was tangible, something you could hold in your hands, or perhaps it was a moment of warmth, an apology, or sustained careful listening to you. Whatever it was, how did it feel? Probably pretty good.

Well, if you are giving . . . toward yourself . . . it's a two-for-one deal! Additionally, there is the built-in bonus that you are taking action, rather than being passive. This helps reduce any "learned helplessness"—a sense of futility and defeat, that there's little you can do to make things better—which studies show is easy to develop and a slippery slope into depression. Another bonus is treating yourself like you matter, which is especially important if you haven't felt that you mattered enough to other people, perhaps as a child.

Further, when you give more to yourself, you'll have more to offer others, since your own cup runneth over. As people experience greater well-being, they are usually more inclined toward kindness, patience, and cooperation.

How

You can gift yourself in lots of ways, many of them intangible and in small moments in everyday life. For example, as I write this, a simple gift to myself is to lean back from the keyboard, take a breath, look out the window, and relax. It's a doable gift.

Not doing can also be an important gift to yourself: not having that third beer, not staying up late watching TV, not getting drawn into a needless argument, not rushing around while you drive . . .

You can see how many opportunities there are each day to offer yourself simple yet beautiful and powerful gifts. Routinely ask yourself: *What could I give myself right now?* Or: *What do I long for that's in my power to give myself?* Or: *In this relationship, what's the biggest gift I could offer myself?* Then try to actually do it.

Focusing on a longer time frame, ask yourself: *How could I help myself this week? This year?* Even: *This life?* Try to keep listening to the answers, letting them ring and ring again in the open space of awareness.

You could imagine a deeply nurturing being and take some time to be aware of what they are giving to you—and then open to giving this to yourself.

Knowing your own giving heart and what you offer to others, can you extend that heart to yourself? Out of kindness and wisdom, cherishing and support, let your gifts flow to that one being in this world over whom you have the most power and therefore to whom you have the highest duty of care—the one who has your name.

11

Forgive Yourself

Everyone messes up. Me, you, the neighbors, Mother Teresa, Mahatma Gandhi, everybody.

It's important to acknowledge mistakes, feel appropriate remorse, and learn from them so they don't happen again. But most people keep beating themselves up way past the point of usefulness.

There is a kind of inner critic and inner protector inside each of us. The inner critic keeps yammering away, looking for something, anything, to find fault with. It magnifies small failings into big ones, punishes you for things long past, and doesn't credit you for your efforts to make amends.

If you're like me and most people I know, you really need your inner protector to stick up for you: to put your weaknesses and misdeeds in perspective, to highlight your many good qualities alongside your occasional mistakes, to encourage you to get back on the high road if you've gone down the low one, and—frankly—to tell that inner critic to *back off*.

With the support of your inner protector, you can see your faults clearly without fearing that you'll fall into the pit of feeling awful. And you can clean up whatever mess you've made as best you can, and move on. The beneficial purpose of guilt, shame, or remorse is *learning*—not punishment!—so that you don't make that mistake again. Anything that's not about learning is mainly needless suffering. Further, beating yourself up about being "bad" makes it harder for you to be "good," since excessive guilt undermines your energy, mood, and confidence.

Seeing faults clearly, taking responsibility for them with appropriate remorse while making amends as best you can, and then coming to peace about them—this is what I mean by forgiving yourself.

How

Start by picking something relatively small, and then try one or more of the methods below. I've spelled them out in detail, but you could do the essence of these methods in a few minutes or less. Then if you like, work up to more significant issues.

Here we go:

- Start by getting in touch with the feeling of being cared about by someone, such as a friend or partner, spiritual being, pet, or person from your past. Open to the sense that aspects of this being, including the caring for you, have been taken into your own mind as parts of your inner protector.
- Staying with feeling cared about, list some of your many good qualities. You could ask the inner protector what it knows about you. These are facts, not flattery, and you don't need a halo to have good qualities like patience, determination, fairness, or kindness.
- Pick something that you feel guilty about. Acknowledge the facts: what happened, what was in your mind at the time, the relevant context and history, and the results for yourself and others. Notice any facts that are hard to face, such as the look in a child's eyes when you yelled at him, and be especially open

to them; they're the ones that are keeping you stuck. It is always the truth that sets us free.

- Sort what happened into three piles: moral faults, unskillfulness, and everything else. Moral faults deserve *proportionate* guilt, remorse, or shame, as well as correction. But unskillfulness calls for only correction; this point is very important. You might ask others what they think about this sorting, including those you may have wronged, but you alone get to decide what goes into each pile. For example, if you gossiped about someone and embellished a mistake they made, you might decide that the lie in your exaggeration is a moral fault deserving a wince of remorse, but casual gossip is simply unskillful and should be corrected (for example, not done again) without yelling at yourself about it.

- In an honest way, take responsibility for your moral fault(s) and unskillfulness. Say in your mind or out loud (or write): *I am responsible for _____ , _____ , and _____ .* Let yourself *feel* it.

- Then add to yourself: *But I am NOT responsible for _____ , _____ , and _____ .* For example, you are not responsible for the misinterpretations or overreactions of others. Further, simply because someone is bothered or upset with you does not *inherently* mean that you did something wrong. Let the relief of what you are *not* responsible for sink in. The fact that you have the right to decide what you are not responsible for enables you to really own what you *are* responsible for.

- Acknowledge what you have already done to learn from this experience, and to repair things and make amends. Let this sink in. Try to appreciate yourself for all of this. Next, decide what, if anything, remains to be done—inside your own mind or out there in the world—and then do it. Let it sink in that you're doing it, and appreciate yourself for this, too.

- Now check in with your inner protector: Is there anything else you should face or do? Listen to that still, quiet voice of conscience, so different from the pounding scorn of the critic. If you truly know that something remains to be done, then take care of it. But, otherwise, know in your heart that what needed to be learned has been learned, and that what needed to be done has been done.

- Now actively forgive yourself. Say in your mind, out loud, in writing, or perhaps to others statements like these: *I forgive myself for _____ , _____ , and _____ . I have taken responsibility for them and done what I could to make things better.* You could ask the inner protector to forgive you. You could ask others to forgive you, including maybe the person you wronged. Take some time with this step.

- You may need to go through one or more of the steps above again and again to truly forgive yourself, and that's all right. Allow the experience of being forgiven to sink in. You can open up to it in your body and heart, and reflect on how it will help others for you to forgive yourself.

May you be at peace.

Part Two

Warm the Heart

12

Feed the
Wolf of Love

Remember the teaching story in the introduction to this book, that everything depends on what we feed each day? That story about the two wolves always gives me the shivers when I think of it. Who among us does not have both a wolf of love and a wolf of hate in their heart?

I know I do. The wolf of hate shows up when I get angry, disdainful, or domineering. Even if it's only inside my own mind—and sometimes it definitely leaks out!

We've got these two wolves because we *evolved* them. Both were needed to keep our ancestors alive in their small hunter-gatherer groups while competing intensely with other bands for scarce resources. Consequently, genes were passed on that promoted cooperation *inside* a band and aggression *between* bands. The wolf of love and the wolf of hate have become woven into human DNA.

As soon as we view others as "not my tribe," whether it's at home or at work or on the evening news, the wolf of hate lifts its head and looks around for danger. Then if we feel at all threatened or mistreated or desperate, the wolf of hate jumps up and looks for someone to howl at.

While the wolf of hate had a function back in the Stone Age, today it breeds mistrust and anger, ulcers and heart disease, and conflicts with others at home and at work. In an increasingly interconnected world, when we dismiss, fear, or attack "them," it usually comes back to bite "us."

How

Hating the wolf of hate just makes it stronger. Instead, you can control it, and channel its fire into healthy forms of protection and assertiveness. And you can avoid feeding it with fear and anger.

Meanwhile, it's so important to feed the wolf of love. As you develop greater compassion, kindness, and interpersonal skills, you naturally become stronger, more patient, and less annoyed or resentful. This helps you avoid pointless conflicts, treat people better, and be less of a threat to others. Then you'll be more likely to get treated better by *them*.

The wolf of love is for you as well as for other people. You can feed it by befriending yourself, as we've discussed. For example, take in the good of everyday experiences of feeling seen, appreciated, liked, and loved. Have compassion for yourself. Be aware of your own decency and kindness; know that you are basically a good person.

You can also feed it by caring about others in ways we'll explore in the rest of this book. For instance, you can see their suffering and wish them well. You can recognize the good in them. You can take a fundamental stance of non-harming toward all beings. You can let in these experiences and make room for the wolf of love in your heart.

You can see the good in the world, and the good in the future that we can make *together*. While the wolf of hate may dominate the headlines, it is actually the wolf of love that is much more pervasive and powerful. For most of humanity's time on this earth, daily life with others in the band was based on compassion and cooperation—what professor Paul Gilbert has termed *caring and sharing*. This is our birthright, and our possibility.

We feed the wolf of love, in other words, with heart and with hope. We feed it by sustaining our sense of what's good in other people, what's good in ourselves, what's already good in our world, and what could be even better in a world we can build together.

We need to stay strong to do this, and hold onto what we know to be true in spite of the brain's tendency to focus on threats and losses, and in spite of the age-old manipulations of various groups that play on fear and anger—*that feed the wolf of hate*—to get even more wealth and power.

So let's stay strong, and hold onto the good that exists all around us and inside us. Let's stay strong, and hold onto each other.

13

See the Person Behind the Eyes

Imagine a world in which people interacted with each other like ants or fish. Imagine being oblivious to the inner life of others while they remain unmoved by your own.

That's a world without empathy.

Your empathy gives you a sense of the feelings, thoughts, and intentions of other people. Meanwhile, their empathy helps you to "feel felt," in professor Dan Siegel's marvelous phrase. Breakdowns in empathy shake the foundation of a relationship. Just recall a time you felt misunderstood—or, even worse, a time when the other person just didn't care at all about understanding you. Anyone who is vulnerable, such as a child, has a particularly strong need for empathy, and the lack of it is very disturbing.

Empathy is soothing, calming, and bridge-building. When it's present, it's much easier to work through things with each other. Empathy gives you lots of useful information, such as what's most important to someone or what's really bothering them. In my experience as a therapist, poor empathy is the core problem in most troubled relationships. Without it, little good is likely to happen. But when both people have empathy, even the toughest issues can get better.

For example, I had a relative with a big heart but a sometimes pushy personality that drove me a little crazy. Finally, I started to imagine that being with her was like looking at a campfire through a lattice covered with thorny vines. I focused on and had empathy for her genuine love for me that was shining through, and didn't get caught up in the vines. That helped both of us a lot.

Most deeply, when you are empathic, that tells others that they exist for you as a being, not as an It—in Martin Buber's model of relationships—but as a Thou to your I. You are recognizing that there's a person over there behind the eyes, someone who feels pain and pleasure, who struggles and strives and wishes life were easier. This sense of being recognized is usually what people want most; it's more fundamental than whatever issue is on the table.

How

Empathy is completely natural. As we evolved, the brain developed three regions that give us a sense of the inner world of others:

- **Empathy for actions**—*Mirror-like networks*, including in the junction between the *temporal* and *parietal lobes* on the sides of your brain, activate both when you perform an intentional action—such as reaching for a cup—and when you see or simply imagine another person doing the same thing.
- **Empathy for emotions**—A part of the brain called the *insula* (on the inside of the temporal lobes) is involved with self-awareness, including your internal sensations and gut feelings. When you experience, say, sadness, your insula gets more active; when you perceive someone else's sadness, your insula can also activate, giving you a sense "from the inside out" of what they're feeling.
- **Empathy for thoughts**—By the time you were three or four years old, your *prefrontal cortex* (behind the forehead) was

able to make inferences about what other people were thinking and planning. We use these capacities to form what's called
a *theory of mind* about the inner world of other people.

We can develop these innate capacities in simple practical
ways in daily life. Through positive neuroplasticity, as you engage
the underlying neural circuitry of empathy, you can strengthen it.

Foundations of Empathy

Remember that empathy is not agreement or approval. For example, you could have empathy for someone who hurt you or is
irritating; you're not waiving your rights. Nor do you have to solve
another person's problem just because you can empathize with it.
Further, we can have empathy for *positive* states of mind in others,
such as sharing in their happiness about a success at work or the
birth of a grandchild.

You could start by taking a couple of deep breaths, and helping
yourself feel calmer and stronger. Studies have found that, paradoxically, a little sense of detachment can actually help us be more
open and receptive to other people, especially if things are getting
intense. In the old saying, good fences make for good neighbors.

If you're in the middle of a conflict, you'll be more empathic if
you can set aside any angry judgments about the other person, at
least for a while. Try to get a sense of their inner being, maybe
rattled and defensive and acting in ways that are problematic, but
really just yearning for happiness and some way to move forward
in life.

Strengthening Empathy

Start with an attitude of curiosity, especially with people you know well. Then see what happens when you focus on their breathing, posture, gestures, and actions. Imagine what it would feel like to move your own body in similar ways.

Tune into their emotions, including the softer ones underneath forcefully expressed positions or anger. Open up to your own gut feelings, which might be resonating with those of other people. Ask yourself what you would be feeling if you were them.

Be curious about their thoughts, memories, expectations, needs, and intentions. Form little hypotheses in your mind about what might be going on over there. Take into account what you know about their personal history—including with you—and their temperament, priorities, and hot buttons. Get a sense of your own innermost being, and then imagine that core inside the other person: that ongoing awareness, the sense of being alive, the one for whom life is hard sometimes.

Tuning into Faces

Out in the world, people usually don't look very much at the faces around them, and if they look, it's briefly and without really seeing. Close to home, you can grow used to familiar faces and then tune out, make assumptions, or look away because you're uncomfortable with what you might see, such as anger, sadness, or simply boredom with what you're saying. With TV and other media, we're bombarded with faces, and it's easy to feel flooded by them, and increasingly numb or inattentive.

As understandable as this is, we pay a price for it. We miss important information about others, lose out on opportunities for closeness and cooperation, and learn too late about potential problems.

So pay particular attention to their facial expressions (without staring or being invasive). These include seemingly universal signs of six fundamental emotions—happiness, surprise, fear, sadness, anger, and disgust—as well as more culturally and personally specific expressions. (For example, I know that very particular look that crosses my wife's face when she thinks I'm getting too full of myself!) Be aware of quick, subtle micromovements around the eyes; human eyes are more expressive than those of any other species.

Have a sense of receiving, of letting in, of *registering* the other person in a deeper way than usual. Notice any discomfort with this. The sense of connection evoked by empathy may feel so intense that it's unnerving. It can also stir up painful longings for even greater connection, and understandable fears of disappointment, especially if that's happened in your past. Keep remembering that you can let in a strong sense of the other person while still being grounded in yourself, and that your empathy is distinct from any actions that might be appropriate in this relationship, such as setting a firm boundary.

Empathy Out Loud

Much as you can usually feel it when another person is truly empathic, even if they don't say a word, your own empathy doesn't always have to be expressed to make a difference. Still, sometimes it's appropriate to share it, hopefully in natural ways, such as a murmur of sympathy or a simple restatement of what they've said (for instance, *Wow, this is a really complicated situation and stressful for you*). You can check out your sense of what it's like to be that other person with questions such as: *What are you thinking? Were you feeling _____? Did you want _____? Did you feel pulled between _____ and _____?*

Be respectful, not persuasive or prosecutorial. Generally try not to mingle expressions of empathy with asserting your own views or needs; as appropriate, do that part later (and we'll explore how in parts four and five).

Notice how your empathy can change the course of an interaction—perhaps softening it and making it more authentic, and maybe leading to a good resolution more gently and quickly.

If it feels right with someone, you might raise the subject of the degree to which you feel seen and understood—or not—by each other. By being empathic yourself, you'll know better what it is you are asking for.

Fundamentally, we can appreciate empathy and advocate for it. We can stand up for the value of truly recognizing the inner life of the person across the table—or across an ocean. The more that another person seems unlike yourself—perhaps with a different nationality, religion, or lifestyle—the more important it is to have empathy for them. In the world as a whole, empathy can help to stitch the fabric of humanity closer together, using the ancient threads that connected us to friends and family long ago on the Serengeti plains.

14

Have Compassion for Them

We're usually aware of our own suffering, from mild frustration or anxiety to the agony of bone cancer or the anguish of losing a child.

But recognizing the suffering in others—that's not so common. All the news of disaster, murder, and grief can numb us to suffering in our own country and across the globe. Close to home, it's easy to tune out or simply miss the stress and strain, unease and anger, in the people with whom we work or live.

Often what matters most to another person is that someone bears witness to their suffering, that someone just really *gets* it. When this doesn't happen, it creates a wound and a sorrow. And at the practical level, if their suffering goes unnoticed, they're unlikely to get the help they need.

When you don't recognize suffering, that harms you as well. You miss chances to have your heart opened, and miss learning what your impact on others might be. Not recognizing their hurts, exasperations, and worries may make issues fester and grow that could have been resolved early on. The suffering of people ten thousand miles away tells us important things about the troubles that may soon come rippling across our own borders.

Compassion is essentially a heartfelt wish that someone not suffer. It is not agreement, approval, or giving up your own needs and rights. You can have compassion for people who've wronged you while also insisting that they treat you better.

Compassion opens your heart and nourishes others. Those who receive it are more likely to be patient, forgiving, and compassionate with you. Compassion reflects the wisdom that everything is related to everything else, and it naturally draws you into feeling more connected with all things.

How

One time I asked the Buddhist teacher and scholar Gil Fronsdal what he was focusing on in his own practice. He paused, then gave me a big smile and said, "I stop for suffering."

Open to Suffering

Look at the faces of people at work, in a store, or across the dinner table. Notice the weariness, the bracing against life, the wariness, irritability, and tension. Sense the suffering behind the words. Feel in your body what it would be like for you to have the life of the other person.

Be careful not to be overwhelmed. You can take this in small doses, even a few seconds at a time. If it helps, bring to mind the sense of being with people who care about you.

Then open again to the suffering of others. To a child who feels like an afterthought, a couple caught up in anger, a coworker passed over for a promotion. Don't glide over faces on the evening news; see the suffering in the eyes looking back at you.

Watch and listen to those closest to you. What's hurting over there? Try to stop for their suffering, even if you have to admit that you are one of its causes. If appropriate, ask some questions, and talk about the answers.

How does it feel to open to suffering? You could find that it brings you closer to others, and that there is more kindness coming back your way. You could feel more grounded in the truth of things, particularly in how it actually is for other people.

Find Compassion

Compassion is natural. You don't have to force it. Just open to the difficulty, the struggle, the stress, the impact of events, the sorrow and strain in the other person. Open your heart, let yourself be moved, and let compassion flow through you.

Sense what compassion is like in your chest and throat and face. Be aware of the way it softens your thoughts and gentles your reactions. Know it so you can find your way back to it again.

Moments of compassion come in the flow of life. Perhaps a friend tells you about a loss, or you can see the hurt behind someone's angry face, or a hungry child looks out at you from the pages of a newspaper. Try to find compassion for people you don't know: someone in a deli, a stranger on a bus, crowds moving down the sidewalk.

You can also explore compassion as a meditative practice, such as the one that follows.

Relax and be aware of your body. Remember the feeling of being with someone who cares about you.

Bring to mind someone it is easy to feel compassion for. Find the sincere wish that they not suffer, perhaps with feelings of concern and caring. If you like, put your compassion into soft thoughts, such as: *May you not suffer . . . May this hard time pass . . . May your sorrow ease . . . May you be at peace with this pain.*

Then expand your circle of compassion to include others. One after another, consider a benefactor (someone who has been kind to you), a friend, a neutral person, and a challenging person. Starting with the benefactor, try to find compassion for each one of these people. Find what you can offer authentically, not forcing anything that feels false or out of reach. If you can't bring sincere compassion to a particular person, that's OK and you can move on to someone who is easier for you.

See if you can extend compassion to all the people in your family . . . neighborhood . . . city . . . state . . . country . . . and world. All the people—right or wrong, liked or disliked, known or unknown—omitting none.

Going further, can you include all of life in your circle of compassion? All the animals, all the plants, even all the microbes. Vast numbers of beings . . . large or small, seen or unseen . . .

Let compassion settle into the background of your mind and body, present in your gaze and words and actions. Omitting none.

15

See the Good in Others

Many interactions these days have a kind of bumper-car quality to them, as we sort of bounce off each other while exchanging information, smiling or frowning, and moving on. How often do we take the extra few seconds to get a sense of what's inside other people—especially their good qualities?

In fact, because of the brain's negativity bias, we're more likely to notice the *bad* qualities in others rather than the good ones: the things that worry or annoy us, or make us critical.

Unfortunately, if you think you're surrounded by lots of bad or at best neutral qualities in others, and only a sprinkling of dimly sensed good ones, you might naturally feel less optimistic and supported. Plus, in a circular way, when other people get the feeling that you don't really see much that's good in them, they are less likely to take the time to see much that's good in you.

Seeing the good in others is thus a simple and powerful way to feel happier, more confident, and more at ease with other people.

How

Slow Down

Step out of the bumper car and spend a few moments being curious about the good qualities in the people in your life. This is *not* looking through rose-colored glasses. You're just taking off the smog-colored glasses of the negativity bias and seeing what the facts really are.

See Abilities

Going through school, I was very young and routinely picked last for teams in PE: not good for anyone's self-esteem. Then, during my first year at UCLA, I gave intramural touch football a try. We had a great quarterback who was just too small for Division I college football. After one practice, he told me in passing, "You're good and I'm going to throw to you more." I was floored. But this was the beginning of me realizing that I was actually a decent athlete. His recognition made me play better, which helped our team. Fifty years later, I can still remember his comment. He had no idea of its impact, yet it was a major boost to my sense of self-worth. In the same way, unseen ripples can spread far and wide when we see abilities in others—especially if we acknowledge them openly.

See Positive Character Traits

Unless you're surrounded by deadbeats and sociopaths—unlikely!—the people you know must have many virtues, such as determination, generosity, kindness, patience, energy, grit, honesty, fairness, or compassion. Take a moment to observe virtues in others. You could make a list of virtues in key people in your life—even in those who are challenging for you.

Find Things to Like

People are like a mosaic. Usually, most of their "tiles" are positive, while some are neutral or negative. Over time, we get used to what's positive and gradually tune it out. Meanwhile, whatever is negative moves to the foreground and stands out. You can observe this happening even with people you love. Some years ago, I realized that I was doing this with my wife, so I started deliberately looking for things to like about her. (She's pretty great, so it wasn't that hard!) It made me happy to do this, and it was good for our relationship.

Try this yourself with friends and family, coworkers, even strangers in a restaurant. Perhaps you can tell that they have a basic decency, a gentleness with children, a plucky passion for doomed causes, or a quirky sense of humor: Can you like these things about them?

Then, for a challenge, try this with someone who is troublesome for you, such as a meddling relative or a frustrating person at work. You're not ignoring what you don't like. In fact, seeing what is good about that person can make interacting with them feel less stressful, which helps if you have to deal with any issues.

Overall, seeing the good in others offers a powerful lesson, that much of how we experience life is based on what we see in it, and that we have the power to see much that is good—for our own sake and that of others.

16

Appreciate
Their Deeper Desires

I did my PhD dissertation by videotaping twenty mother-toddler pairs and analyzing what happened when the mom offered an alternative to a problematic desire ("Not the sharp knife, sweetie. How about these big spoons?!"). Hundreds of bleary-eyed hours later, I found that providing alternatives reduced negative emotions in children and increased their cooperation with parents.

I was glad about this result, both as a new parent and as someone desperate to finish grad school. Kids—and adults, too—obviously want to get what they desire from others. But it's more important to know that others actually recognize our desires—and even more fundamentally, that they *want* to.

Consider any significant relationship: someone at work, or a friend, or a family member. How does it feel when they misinterpret your goals, intentions, or requests? Or worse, when they apparently don't care about simply *understanding* what it is that you'd like, what you care about, what is important to you?

Ouch.

Turn it around: When you recognize the deeper desires of others, they are more likely to feel seen and understood. And it becomes easier to ask them to do the same for you.

A key aspect of this is seeing their underlying good intentions. One time, hustling through an airport, I stopped to buy some water. At the shop's refrigerator, a man was bent over, loading bottles into it. I reached above him and pulled out one he'd just put in.

He glanced up, stopped working, got a bottle from another shelf, and held it out to me, saying briskly, "This one is cold." For a few seconds I thought he was telling me I'd done something wrong. Then I understood that he was trying to be helpful: He'd realized that I'd gotten a warm bottle, and he cared enough to shift gears and get me a cold one. In a simple way, he wished me well. I said thanks and took the one he offered. It was just a bottle of water. But I felt touched by his good intentions.

It may be hard to recognize the good wishes in others. The brain reacts to novelty, so it tends to ignore the many positive intentions that pervade most daily life while spotlighting the occasional negative ones.

So you have to actively *look* for the underlying positive intentions and desires in others. Then you'll find them all around you.

How

With a friend or a stranger, look for their deeper desires beneath the surface. You might find a wish for pleasure, a commitment to others, a priority on security, a delight in life, a valuing of autonomy, or a need for love.

Look down into yourself and you'll find many of the same longings. They're just as powerful and precious to the other person as they are to you.

Deep down, most wants are positive. The *means* to these ends may be misguided, but the fundamental *ends* themselves are usually good ones. Even horrible behaviors can be misguided efforts to gain positive things like pleasure, status, or control. Of course, recognizing underlying good intentions does not justify bad behavior.

If you like, consider something you did that you regret. What positive aims were your actions trying to serve? What's it like to recognize this? Seeing the good aims underlying bad actions can soften defensiveness and help move a person to appropriate remorse, and to greater resolve to find better ways to pursue those aims.

When you're talking with friends, be aware of their deeper desires. How does it feel to recognize them? Try this routinely with people you care about. Doing this will help you understand them better and feel closer to them. You could also look for positive motivations in people you don't know. You'll see efforts to do a good job, loyalty to friends and causes, fair play, helpfulness, and many other good things.

Try this with people who are difficult for you. Try to see their deeper wants, beneath what has bothered or hurt you. When you recognize their underlying positive aims, you might be able to find less harmful ways that the person could use to fulfill them.

There's an ember of goodness in each one of us, including the one looking back in the mirror. Recognizing positive intentions blows on that ember and helps it grow into a warm and beautiful flame.

17

Be Kind

We can be kind in many ways, such as a friendly hello, opening a door for a stranger, a warm glance, a smile, or inviting someone else to speak in a meeting. Compassion means that we don't want other beings to suffer, and kindness means that we want them to be happy.

With kindness, we *approach* the world rather than withdrawing from it, which studies have shown to be associated with positive mood, realistic optimism, and success. As we've seen in part one, kindness to yourself enables you to sustain kindness to others. Kindness to me is kindness to you, and kindness to you is kindness to me, in a lovely upward spiral. The opposite is also true: Harming yourself harms others, and harming others harms you, in a painful downward spiral. Kindness neutralizes ill will, the wish that others suffer. It encourages other people to be less guarded or reactive with you, since you're answering the ancient question—friend or foe?—with an open hand and an open heart.

How

Sometimes it may not feel possible, authentic, or appropriate to be kind, such as with someone who's attacking you or might misinterpret your friendliness. Otherwise, we can be kind with all sorts of people, including intimates and strangers, coworkers and in-laws, babies and bosses. We can be kind toward nonhuman animals, even toward the Earth itself. People have different styles, and that's all right. The gruff kindness of my relatives in North Dakota is different from the touchy-feely kindness of my therapist friends in California—but the heart is the same.

Be for Them

We normally tend to be pretty preoccupied with ourselves. Kindness shifts that focus, at least for a while, to other people.

Some years ago, I was invited to give a keynote address at a conference with the largest audience I'd ever faced. It was a big step up for me. Legendary psychologists were giving the other talks, and I feared I wouldn't measure up. I was nervous. Real nervous.

I sat in the back waiting my turn, worrying about how people would view me. Would they think I was just a big imposter? I thought about different ways to look impressive and get their approval. My mind fixated on me, me, me. I was miserable.

Searching for a distraction, I saw a newsletter sitting on a nearby chair. I picked it up and found an interview with the Dalai Lama. He spoke about the happiness in wishing others well and being of service to them. He was inspiring, and I felt a wave of calm as I stopped obsessing about "me" and just rested in the feeling of wanting to be helpful.

So I gave my talk, and stayed focused on what could be useful to the people in the audience, rather than how I was coming across. I felt much more relaxed and at peace—and, to my surprise, got a standing ovation. Later, I laughed to myself at the ironies: To get approval, stop seeking it; to take care of yourself, take care of others.

Cultivate Kindness

Kindness is natural. Still, you can strengthen it as a trait inside yourself. You could bring to mind a time when you were particularly kind to someone, and be aware of the feelings and attitudes you had toward that person, and what you said and did; let the sense of all this sink into you, becoming a part of you. With others, you can build the habit of leaning forward a little, rather than back; softening and opening your chest, face, and eyes; and breathing goodwill in and out.

Try thinking gently to yourself things like this: *May you be happy . . . may you live with ease . . . may you be healthy . . . may you be successful . . . may you find the love you long for . . .* Alongside these thoughts, invite feelings of warmth and friendliness; get a sense of opening your heart. Explore what different aspects of kindness feel like, such as being considerate . . . helpful . . . generous . . . friendly . . . courteous . . . well-meaning . . . humane . . . supportive . . . appreciative . . . or affectionate. Be aware of how these aspects of kindness can feel fulfilling and enjoyable, which will help to hardwire the trait of kindness into your nervous system.

If you like, take some time with this as a meditation, starting with someone you easily feel kind toward. Next, explore good wishes toward people who are more neutral for you, such as a distant acquaintance at work or a neighbor down the street. Then see if you can extend genuine kindness toward someone who is challenging for you; you might find that this actually helps you feel less stressed or upset with them, and more effective in the actions you choose to take. Finish the meditation with a general sense of warmheartedness and benevolence as simply a way of being, applied to everyone.

Overall, notice that your kindness is more about you than it is about other people, more about how you approach the world than what you find there.

Deliberately Express It

Look for opportunities for little acts of kindness in everyday life. Often, you'll just give a smile, a handshake, or a nod—and that's plenty. Maybe it's offering a few minutes to talk. Or a morning hug or a good-night kiss. Or an extra touch of warmth in an email.

You can stretch yourself while staying within the range of what feels genuine to you. Remember that kindness is not agreement or approval. You can be kind to people while still pursuing your own goals, even ones that are different from theirs. You can wish people well while still having issues with them.

Consider the people who are close to you. For example, having worked with couples for many years, it's painful to see how often basic friendliness is a casualty in a long-term relationship. Consider being kinder toward parents, siblings, or your children if you have them. Again, it's startling how easily this can be crowded out of our most important relationships by busyness, little irritations and hurts, or weariness from working too hard. But bits of kindness, sprinkled here and there, can be absolutely transformational in a relationship. Try it and see!

Consider being kinder toward people you might normally ignore or treat with distance, even coolness, such as waitstaff in restaurants, someone shuttling you to the airport, or customer service people on the phone.

You can be pressed and stressed and still be kind. Find your warmth and good wishes amid the mental clutter, like hearing wind chimes amid storm and rain. Over time, you'll have a growing sense of *being* kindness. Really! It will be where you come from, your foundation and natural inclination. See what happens when you add one small log after another, fueling that warm glowing fire on the hearth in your heart.

18

Put No One
Out of Your Heart

We all know people who are, ah, . . . *challenging*. It might be a bossy supervisor, a nice but flaky friend, a coworker who is frankly a pain in the neck, or a partner you're struggling with. Ironically, in order for good relationships to be *so* nurturing to us as human beings, we must be so linked to others that some of them can really rattle us. Then it's natural to close off to them, often with hurt, resentment, or scorn. But what are the results? Closing off feels tense and contracted, and it primes us to be more emotionally reactive, which might make matters worse.

Sometimes you do have to hang up the phone, block someone on Facebook, or stay at a motel when visiting relatives. In extreme situations, it may be necessary to distance yourself completely from another person for a while or forever. Take care of yourself, and listen to that inner knowing about what's best for you. You may have to put someone out of your business, work group, holiday party list—or bed.

But whatever practical steps you need to take, you can still ask yourself: *Do I have to put this person out of my heart?*

How

When your heart is open, what's that like? Physically, does it feel like warmth and relaxation in your chest? What's it like emotionally? You might feel a sense of empathy, compassion, and calm.

What's it like mentally, such as keeping things in perspective and having good intentions?

Feel the strength in being openhearted, wholehearted, large-hearted. Paradoxically, the most open and seemingly vulnerable person in a relationship often ends up being the strongest one.

Get a sense of your heart being expansive and inclusive, like the sky. The sky stays open to all clouds, and it isn't harmed by even the stormiest ones. Keeping your heart open actually makes it harder for others to upset you.

Notice that a spacious heart still allows for clarity about what works for you and what doesn't, as well as firmness, lines in the sand, and straight talk. Mahatma Gandhi, Nelson Mandela, and the Dalai Lama are famous for keeping their hearts open while being *very* effective with their adversaries.

Open Your Heart

Make a commitment to an open, spacious heart. Commit to not exiling others from your circle of compassion. Commit to never making another person "dead to me."

Be mindful of what it feels like—physically, emotionally, mentally—to have cast a particular person out of your heart. Be aware of the rationalizations and reasons the reactive brain/mind throws up to justify this—and ask yourself: *Are these true? Are they necessary? Are they consistent with the kind of person I want to be?* Be aware of any pain you've suffered—or seen inflicted on others—from this person, and bring compassion to it.

Next, ask yourself, given the realities of this challenging person, how could you protect yourself without putting them out of your heart? For example, it might help to:

- Get some physical or emotional distance.
- Set a strong boundary, such as refusing to talk when they're obviously drunk.
- Vent to a friend and get some things off your chest so you can release them.
- Talk to the challenging person, if only to know that you've said and done what you could.
- Remind yourself that you can have a simple, heartfelt sense of your shared humanness with someone you never ever want to see again.

Then if you're willing, explore opening your heart again to those you've cast out of it. Nothing might change in your behavior or in the nature of the relationship. Nonetheless, you'll *feel* different—and better.

"Us" All "Thems"

Now I'd like to look at large-heartedness in a broader context. For several million years, our ancestors survived by caring about those inside their band—"us"—while often fearing and attacking others outside the band—"them." That's a long, long time. Then during the last ten thousand years, as agriculture produced food surpluses that enabled larger groups, this same tribalistic pattern has been repeated at bigger scales. Consequently, most of us are vulnerable to the ancient drumbeats of grievance and vengeance—now amplified to a thunder by social media.

And it's not just in our politics. You can see the "them-ing" of others in the rapid mental sorting of people into like-me and not-like-me. You can see it in office gossip and family discord. The in-group and the out-group, the casual dismissals, the turning away in anger, the easy disdain. You can watch your mind moving quickly to reduce another person to a two-dimensional figure as you invest in your own position and identity—even when that person is your beloved partner.

This process of making others into a "them" is shaped by broad forces of prejudice and discrimination that have a long and painful history, and which continue to be institutionalized and enacted today—perhaps experienced by a woman facing a glass ceiling at work or a young Black man hearing car doors lock as he strolls down a sidewalk.

In ways large and small, you probably know what it's like to feel "them-ed" yourself. To be ignored, discounted, used, attacked, or tossed aside. Not good at all.

On the other hand, to "us" others is to see what we have in common—to recognize that all of *us* want pleasure and fear pain, that we all suffer and die, that each of us will be separated one way or another from everything and everyone we love someday. As you see this fact and the deep ways in which we are all alike, a wary tension in the body can ease. Then you will see others more clearly and be more effective in dealing with them, even those you oppose fiercely. And when you don't feel needlessly threatened, you're less likely to be needlessly threatening yourself.

As you move through your day, recognize similarities between yourself and others. For example, when you see someone you don't know, take a dozen seconds to really look at them and get a sense of them: *Yes, they're like me . . . Their back hurts just as mine does . . . They love their kids just as I do . . . They, too, have felt joy and sorrow.* Try this in particular with people who seem very different from you, and with people who belong to groups you may mistrust or fear or dislike. Notice what this practice feels like for you—probably heart-opening and calming.

You could imagine a kind of circle of "us" that includes you and others who are obviously like you. Then gradually widen that circle to include more and more people who at first seem unlike you, but with whom you can recognize similarities (for example, like me, you want to be happy). Keep widening the circle to include people who have harmed you or others, knowing that you don't have to approve of them to recognize our shared humanity. Take your time with this, drawing on compassion for yourself and others, and expanding the circle only as it feels true and right for you. Be aware of a softening in yourself as you do this, a releasing of defensiveness and righteousness, a widening of your perspective. Rest in how this feels, and enjoy it.

It's in these ways that bridges are built among us, and circles widen, and we can live together in peace.

19

Trust in Love

Love in all its forms is like air. It might be hard to see—but it's in you and all around you. Daily life is full of moments of co-operation and generosity, even between complete strangers. Many scientists believe that love—defined broadly to include empathy, friendship, altruism, romance, compassion, and kindness—has been the primary driving force behind the evolution of the brain over the last several million years.

The resting state of your brain—its "home base" when you are not stressed, in pain, or feeling threatened—encourages a sense of love. Nonetheless, it's all too easy to be driven from home by something as small as a critical comment in a business meeting or a frown across a dinner table. Then we go off to a kind of inner homelessness, caught up in the fear or anger that leaves love behind. After a while, this can become the new normal, and then we call homelessness home—like forgetting the richness of air that would be available if we would only breathe deeply.

So we need to come home to love. You can recognize and have confidence in the love in your own heart, which will energize and protect you, even when you must be assertive with others. You can see and have faith in the love in others, even when it is veiled or it comes out in problematic ways. You can trust in love that's as present as air, and trust in loving that's as natural as breathing.

How

Take a breath. Notice how available air is, how you can trust in it. Notice the feeling of being able to rely on the air.

Then think of someone who loves you. *Feel* the fact of this love—even if it is, to paraphrase the psychologist John Welwood, a perfect love flowing through an imperfect person. Can you feel your breath and body relaxing, as you trust in this person's love for you? Can you feel your thoughts calming, your mood improving, and your heart opening to others? Let it sink in, that trusting in love feels good and refuels you. Try this again with other people who love you.

Call to mind someone *you* love. Feel the reality of your love; know that you are loving. As in the previous paragraph, absorb the benefits of recognizing and trusting in your love. Try this with others you love.

As you go through your day, open to your own lovingness in different situations. You could ask yourself questions like these: *As a loving person, what is important to me here? Trusting in love, what seems like the right thing to do?* Remember that you can be strong while staying centered in love or one of its many expressions (for instance, empathy, fair play, goodwill). If you need to assert yourself, what happens when you do so from a loving place?

Let Your Love Flow

In my early twenties, I went through Rolfing, a form of deep-tissue bodywork that can sometimes release buried emotional material, and I nervously anticipated the fifth session, the one that goes deep into the belly. But instead of gobs of repressed pain, what poured out was *love*—waves and waves of love that I'd pushed down due to embarrassment, fears of closeness, and my struggles with my mother.

It felt fantastic to let it flow freely. Love nurtures and heals us as it moves through us. In fact, wounds from not *receiving* love are soothed and sometimes even healed by *giving* love.

Love is a natural upwelling current inside us all. It doesn't need to be pushed or pumped, it just needs to be released. If love is bottled up, it hurts. In your important relationships, are there any ways in which you're withholding or watering down your love?

Choose to Love

Many years ago, my romantic partner at the time started doing things that shocked and hurt me. I won't be specific, but it was intense. After going through the first wave of reactions—*Wha?! How could you? Are you kidding me?!*—I settled down a bit. I had a choice.

This relationship was important to me, and I could see that most of what was going through her mind was about her and not me. I realized that I could tell her that we were on very thin ice . . . and choose to love in the meantime. Considering everything, this felt like the freest, strongest, and most self-respecting thing I could do.

To my surprise, instead of turning me into a doormat or punching bag, love actually protected and fueled me. It kept me out of contentiousness and conflict, and gave me a feeling of self-worth. I was interested in what she was ultimately going to do, but in a weird way I didn't care that much. I felt fed and carried by love, and what she did was out of my hands. Gradually, my shift away from trying to change her and toward being loving myself helped things get better.

Love is more about us being loving than about other people being lovable. It may be frustrating to try to get others to love you. But no one can stop you from finding and feeling love inside yourself. You can choose to "love at will," and come from the upper end of the range of what is authentically available to you. Whatever this range is at any moment in a relationship, it's your choice where you land within it. This is not phony; the love you feel is real. In fact, choosing to love is twice loving: It's a loving act to call up the intention to love, plus there is the love that follows.

Let love be there alongside whatever else is present in your relationship with the other person. There is love . . . and there is also seeing what is true about the other person, yourself, and circumstances affecting both of you. There is love . . . and there is taking care of your own needs in the relationship. Love first, and the rest will follow.

If you're stuck in a really bad situation—perhaps a chronic health problem or painful loss—what can you do when there's nothing you can do? You can always find someone to love.

See the Love in Others

You can tune into the love in others, no matter how obscured by their own inner homelessness, their own fear or anger—like seeing a distant campfire through the trees. Sense the longing in people to be at peace in their relationships, and to give and get love. What happens in a challenging relationship when you stay in touch with this capacity and desire for love inside the other person, even if it's bottled up? Notice that you can both feel the lovingness in others *and* be direct and clear about your own rights and needs.

Trusting in love does not mean assuming that someone will love you. It means having confidence in the underlying loving nature of every person, and in the wholesome power of your own lovingness to protect you and touch the heart of others.

Be Lived by Love

Fundamentally, you can feel *lived* by love. Love as a current, a wellspring, an updraft that is living through you and carrying you along. Kindness, compassion, and other forms of love can be the central movement of your life. In both meditation and daily activities, try to feel that you are breathing love in and breathing love out. You might even feel that love is breathing *you* in and out . . . perhaps thinking softly: *loving in . . . loving out . . .*

Bring this down to earth: If you lived from love in your first encounter with another person today, how would you be, what would you do, how would you speak? What would a week, a year, be like in which you were lived by love?

Love will bring us home.

Part Three

Be at Peace
with Others

20

Take It Less Personally

Imagine that you and a friend are in a canoe on a gently flowing river. You're dressed up in nice clothes and having a Sunday picnic. Suddenly there's a loud THUMP on the side of the canoe and it tips over. The water is cold and you come up sputtering. What do you see? Two teenagers are laughing at you because they snuck up and dumped you in the river. How do you feel?

Now imagine this scenario again: the friend and the canoe, the nice clothes and the picnic, the loud THUMP and getting dumped into the cold river. What do you see when you come up sputtering? This time, a large submerged log has crashed into your canoe. How do you feel?

And what is the difference in how you feel in the two scenarios?

In the second one, the shock, the cold water, and the ruined picnic are the same as the first—but you don't feel personally targeted. You might feel stressed and irritated without needing to personalize any of it. It's just a crummy situation and you cope with it and learn from it. You don't ruminate about the mean log.

Most of the people who bump into us are like logs. What they say and do was set in motion by many, many impersonal causes and conditions upstream of this moment, such as their personal history and external forces in society. We need to deal with their impacts on us, but we will suffer less and be more effective if we take it less personally.

For example, I grew up in Los Angeles and have driven many miles with a good safety record. My wife, Jan, is a *very* cautious driver, and prefers me to do the driving on the freeway. We'd often be rolling along steadily while staying far back from the car in front of us . . . and still her hand would be white-knuckling the passenger door and her foot would be mashing an imaginary brake pedal to the floor while she told me sharply to slow down.

I took it personally.

My parents were loving, but still quite critical in various ways. I learned to drive with my dad and he was pretty intense about it. So I was prone, many years later, to feeling unfairly blamed and scolded, including about driving.

After multiple rounds of flaring back at my wife (which never ended well), I started thinking about it. Was I actually driving dangerously? Nope. Did I have to believe what she was saying? No again. On the other hand, could I have compassion for her? Definitely. She's someone I love, and I don't want to upset her for the sake of arriving somewhere five minutes sooner. Could I recognize some of the factors behind her reactions *that were not about me*, such as little freeway experience, not-great depth perception, and a vulnerable spine that absolutely must avoid any kind of accident? Absolutely! In other words, could I see things more impersonally and just focus on what would improve our situation? These reflections helped me shift into driving more slowly when she's in the car. I don't always do this when I'm alone, but it's sure been good for our relationship.

How

Take Care of Yourself

When we're tired, stressed, or hungry, it's sure a lot easier to feel put-upon, picked on, or offended. On the other hand, *the better you take care of yourself as a person, the less you'll take things personally*. Simple things like getting enough sleep and finding something to enjoy each day can make a big difference. Then what others do is less likely to feel like a personal injury.

In particular, we have a deep natural need to feel seen and appreciated by others. In childhood, this need is intense, and if there was a shortfall in these "social supplies" from your parents, siblings, and other kids, you're left with a kind of hole in the heart (this certainly happened for me). Then in adulthood, you could be prone to feeling misunderstood, left out, or slighted. Maybe the other person really did mistreat you, but it's so easy to overreact to it and take it painfully personally.

To help yourself with this, deliberately look for and take in experiences of feeling cared about and valued. Bit by bit, synapse by synapse, you really can fill that hole in your heart. Then when others land on you, it will feel like you have a big shock absorber inside. They're still doing whatever they're doing, but now you can see that it's more about them than about you.

Recognize Assumptions about Others

A key idea from psychology is that we routinely *attribute* characteristics to others, such as a hostile attitude or the deliberate intention to be hurtful. Sometimes these attributions are wrong, overstated, or just part of a much larger picture.

Think about a recent upset with someone or a challenging relationship in general. What characteristics have you attributed to the other person, even automatically? Have you "transferred" how people have treated you in the past to this other person—for example, thinking that they are like your mother or father, or some horrible coach or boss you once had?

A simple but powerful exercise is to create two columns on a piece of paper. On the left side, list some key attributions about someone; on the right side, for each attribution, list any ways that it is not entirely true. For example, I might have listed that my wife was "bossy" while I was driving, plus acting like my critical father. Then in the right-hand column I would write that she was actually just feeling scared, plus, in general, she is nurturing and appreciative.

Our attributions are usually quick, dogmatic, and lurking in the background of the mind. It is freeing to become aware of them. You can decide what is actually true—or not.

In particular, we react strongly to the *intentions* we attribute to others, including their motivations, values, and goals. Think about children yelling at each other: "You did it on purpose!" But much of the time we are just bit players in other people's dramas, bumping into their bad day. Even if there was some conscious intention behind what they did to you, it might well be a minor and passing reaction from them and not part of a broad plan to target and hurt you. And they might have other intentions toward you, including good ones. Without denying what is actually true about the deliberate behavior of another person, try saying things like this to yourself:

Underneath it all, your motivations are basically good.

You acted in that problematic way because deep down you want _____ .

You got triggered and reactivated and, yes, acted badly—but it's not because you've got some big elaborate agenda to hurt me.

Hmm, I misinterpreted what you meant and why you said it, and I can appreciate that you had a positive intention to

_____ *.*

When you get anxious, you do get controlling, but I can understand this as coming out of your fear and not as a criticism of me; plus, much of the time you're not anxious.

Know What You're Going to Do

Taking things less personally does *not* mean letting yourself be mistreated or abused. It may happen that someone has deliberately targeted you. It may even be part of a larger societal pattern of prejudice and discrimination. As a cisgender, heterosexual white male, I've had the advantage of being able to avoid the biases that target and disadvantage so many others. Still, perhaps like you as well, I've been lied about, lied to, robbed, and betrayed. It's real. It hurts, it's scary, and it's something you have to deal with.

As we've explored, you can bring compassion to yourself, find a sense of calm strength, and know that your own worth is independent of that other person. You could deliberately get in touch with experiences that are a kind of antidote or balm, such as remembering people who have praised you if your work was unfairly attacked in a meeting. You could reach out to a friend for support and perspective. You could come to a considered view about the motives and other forces inside the other person. You could make your own judgment about the scale of what happened, from a minor affront to a devastating injury. You could choose to talk with that person, drawing on the approaches in parts four and five of this book.

And whether you speak with them or not, you can know for yourself what your plan is from this point forward. You can see events in a more impersonal, big-picture way, while protecting yourself and pursuing your own goals. Perhaps you decide to invest more time in other friendships, end a romantic relationship, shift to another manager at work, or simply stay civil while seeing clearly what sort of person they are.

It's calming and centering to know what you're going to *do*. To return to where we began, you can deal with being dumped in the water, and keep a sharper eye out for logs in the future, and even choose some different rivers—all while taking things less personally.

21

Get Out of the War in Your Head

Sometimes we get caught up in hostile, resentful, even vengeful thoughts and feelings toward another person. In the mind, it's like we've gone to war with them. No bombs or missiles, but a chronic conflict and angry feelings. It could be colleagues arguing about a project, romantic partners edging toward a breakup, or divorced parents continuing to battle over holidays. It might be a cold war of polite behavior, chilly silences, and quiet seething. In my own internal wars with others, I became preoccupied with rehashing events, imagining what I would really say if I could, and wishing that others would stand up for me. I was stuck in a fight. But mainly I was harming myself.

When I was sixteen, I worked at a summer camp next to the Pacific Ocean, and we would go skin diving around the forests of kelp. One time I foolishly swam into a thicket of kelp, thinking there was clear water just on the other side, but there was only more seaweed, with thick orangish leaves and long strong vines reaching up from the seabed below. I was trapped, running out of air, and began to panic. I battled the kelp, thrashing and jerking, which only wrapped it more tightly around me. After I don't know how long, a clarity came over me and my war with the kelp ended. The diving mask was around my throat, the snorkel ripped out of my mouth, and I'd lost a fin. I slowly disentangled myself from the kelp, rather than fighting it, working my way upward, finally clearing it, seeing the bright silver surface of the ocean above my head, and rising up to it and then the precious air.

We certainly need to stand up for ourselves and deal with tough things. But if we do this while caught in anger, like a swimmer caught in kelp, that's not good for us or others. A mind at war feels bad, full of irritation and fear. The body revs up, accumulating the gradual wear and tear of stress activation. Perceptions and beliefs get biased and defended. Reactions are intensified and accelerated. All this can lead others to go to war with *you*, driving vicious cycles.

How

Think about any kind of tension or conflict you might have with someone. It could be in the present, or in the past with people who make you angry when you think of them.

Mental Factors

No matter what they've done, however bad it's been, try to be aware of the *mental factors* that may have gotten *added* to the situation and keep you stuck in this fight:

- Are there any emotional payoffs, such as feeling right, self-righteous, or superior? If so, ask yourself if these rewards are worth the costs.
- Are your reactions keeping at bay softer feelings of hurt or sadness? If so, try to explore these underlying feelings with compassion, accept them, let them flow, and gradually become less swept along by anger.

- Does staying in this fight make you feel entitled to demand things from others (for example, now they "owe" you)? If so, consider how your rights and needs are legitimate without you requiring any added claims on others to justify them. Imagine speaking up for your rights and needs in and of themselves without putting them in the frame of your grievances with others.

Familiar Scripts

Consider how your approach to conflict has been shaped by your upbringing and life experiences. In my own family, my parents bickered a lot about the same issues over and over again, so I didn't really have models of actually *resolving* conflicts—which is much of what this book is about—until I left home and got involved with the human potential movement and then clinical psychology. In other families, conflicts could be resolved by somebody being dominating, while those who must acquiesce are outwardly submissive and inwardly resentful. Similar patterns of interacting can happen with other kids during childhood—for example, I was afraid of bullies at school—and then with other adults over time.

These ways of relating become internalized, both in terms of how we act with others—bickering with no resolution? getting pushy? submitting to keep the peace?—and how we feel inside. As you recognize ways you could be enacting familiar "scripts" from your own background, it may feel embarrassing or disheartening. Remind yourself that we are designed to learn from our experiences, and that you are taking a higher road already just through your willingness to be honest with yourself. Simply being aware of these scripts reduces their power over you. It takes time to change them, and you may find yourself still speaking oh-so-familiar lines—as I've done repeatedly before realizing: *Yikes, I'm sounding like my dad again with our kids.* But gradually you'll be able to step out of old scripts, and step into less reactive and more effective ways of handling issues with others.

A Peaceable Mind

Try this little exercise (and feel free to modify it for your own purposes): Draw a line down a page to create two columns, and label the one on the left "Peaceful Strength" and the one on the right "Mind at War." In each column, list the thoughts, feelings, and aims of each way of being. For example, the left side might include "calm, see the big picture, patient, undistracted by side issues" while on the right there's "heart pounding, want them to pay a price, fixated on one thing, pretty unhappy, ruminating, stressed, tense."

Then pause and consider two things. First, you can stick up for yourself—and later chapters will show you how—while being at peace *inside* yourself. They might be at war with you, but the war doesn't need to invade your own mind! You don't have to quarrel with them inside yourself. You don't have to be invaded and occupied by righteousness and antagonism. Fundamentally, you don't have to get swirled along by the mind-streams of other people. Reflect on the neurological turbulence underlying their thoughts: the incredibly complicated, dynamic, and largely arbitrary churning of momentary neural assemblies into coherence and then chaos and then coherence again. Getting upset about somebody's thoughts is like getting upset about spray from a waterfall. Try to decouple your thoughts from those of other people. Tell yourself: *They're over there and I'm over here . . . Their mind is separate from my mind.* Recall someone who embodies this combination of strength and non-reactivity to the warlikeness of others; imagine what they might be thinking and feeling in your situation, and get a sense of this way of being sinking into you.

Second, see how costly mind-at-war is for you and other people, including innocent bystanders, such as children. When I think about my mistakes in this life, in most of them I was caught up in some kind of war in my head. What's the greater good, for both you and others? Maybe let them have their little victory to foster a greater happiness. Make a heartfelt choice for a more peaceable mind.

We can recognize the war inside ourselves, rather than getting drawn into the accusations, positions, threats, and recriminations of others. The world outside may not change. But if you end the war in your own head, you'll feel better and act better. Which just might help the world to change for the better as well.

22

Accept Them

I admit it: I wish some people were different. Depending on who they are, I wish they'd stop doing things like leaving cabinet doors open in our kitchen, sending me spam emails, or turning a blind eye to global warming. And I wish they'd start doing things like being friendlier and more helpful. Even if it doesn't affect me directly, for their own sake I do wish that some people I care about were more energetic, less anxious, or less self-critical.

In what ways do *you* wish that people were different? Think about the people close to you as well as coworkers, neighbors, and drivers on the highway. It's normal to wish that others were different, just as it's normal to wish that you, yourself, were different (say, richer or wiser). It's fine to try to influence others in skillful, ethical ways. But problems come when we tip into fault-finding, badgering, contempt, or any other kind of *struggle*. Instead, we could accept them for who they are, and for who they are not.

Acceptance means you "give up" to the truth—the facts, reality—no matter what it is. You may not like it for understandable reasons. For example, I don't like the facts that many children go hungry each day, that my mother and father are no longer here, and that I've hurt people by losing my temper. But things are what they are, and we can accept them while still trying to make them better, when that's possible. Acceptance grounds us in what is true, which is where we have to start for any lasting effectiveness, happiness, or healing.

Accepting people does *not* itself mean agreeing with them, liking them, or downplaying their impact on you. You can still take appropriate actions. You're simply accepting the reality of the other person. You may not like it, you may not prefer it, you may feel sad or angry about it, but, at a deeper level, you are at peace with it. That alone is a blessing. And, sometimes, your shift to acceptance can open a kind of space in which a relationship can improve.

How

To have a clear experience of acceptance, start with a simple, direct, undeniable experience, such as accepting the sensations of breathing. For a few breaths, focus on the sense of letting the breath be whatever it is. Try saying softly in your mind things like these: *I accept this rising of the chest . . . I accept this falling . . . this flowing in and flowing out. I accept that there is breathing now . . . I accept the fact of breathing now . . .* Try taking it a little further: *I accept the fact that this body needs air . . . I accept that I need to breathe.*

What does acceptance feel like? What is enjoyable or meaningful about it?

Accepting What's Hard to Accept

Now try something that is hard to accept, starting with a small to medium issue. Some examples might be: *I can't believe that some people don't use their turning signals while driving . . . I don't like how my roommate does the dishes . . . I wish my partner were less hyper-rational and more in touch with their feelings.*

Then, just as you did for breathing, try to hold this fact in a context of acceptance. Fill in the blank with the fact, and say things to yourself like these: *It's true that _____ . . . I see that _____ . . . I surrender to the fact that _____ . . . I wish with all my heart that _____ weren't the case, but it is . . . I give up about _____ . . . I accept _____ .* See if you can soften around the truth of things, if you can open out to the way things are.

Understanding Blocks to Acceptance

As you try to be more accepting of others, you might bump into two common blocks.

The first block is avoiding the disappointment or even despair you could feel if you really got that someone was just that certain way, and likely to stay that way. Remind yourself that you can tolerate these painful feelings as they pass through awareness while finding a deeper acceptance of the reality of the other person.

The second block is pushing to make something happen that just won't. For example, while it may be sad to face it, it might simply be true that someone will never admit what they did or give you the love you long for. Our strengths, not just our weaknesses, can get us in trouble, such as being so determined that you keep searching too long inside tunnels that truly have no cheese. After you've let yourself feel understandable frustration and regret, imagine putting your energy where there is more support and possibility.

Fully Accepting Someone

Pick a person who is important to you. (You can do this practice with multiple people.) In your mind, out loud, or in writing, say things like these and see how you feel: *I accept you completely . . .*

Countless causes, large and small, have led you to think, speak, and act the way you do . . . You are who you are . . . I let it be . . . You are a fact and I accept the facts in my life . . . You and I are part of a larger whole that is what it is, and I accept that, too.

If you like, be more specific, naming aspects of this person that particularly bother you, such as: *I accept that you snore . . . are always late . . . leave your clothes on the floor . . . are still angry at me . . . have little natural interest in sex . . . are fighting me tooth-and-nail in this divorce . . . don't really understand me.*

Consider how you may have gotten tangled up with this other person, struggling to change them. When I reflect on this myself, I become aware of my own pushiness, irritability, and hurts. See if you can let go of some, even all, of your own entanglements. Open to the easing and peace that can come when you do.

Consider how much you like it when you feel that another person accepts you completely. It's a beautiful gift—and we can give it ourselves to others when we accept *them*. Imagine how it might improve your relationship with someone if that person felt you accepted them fully. Acceptance is a gift that gives back.

It's easy to accept beautiful sunsets, golden prizes, and warm smiles. It's the hard things that are hard to accept. So it's important to appreciate the peace that comes from giving up the fight with the way it is.

You can still do whatever you can—which might be nothing, unfortunately—while facing what is actually true. This often eases conflicts with others. And at some point an easing can come into your heart, a softening and a clarity. With a hard-won, honest freedom.

23

Relax, You're Going to Be Criticized

The title of this practice is a little tongue-in-cheek. What I mean is, we can spend too much time worrying about criticism. Yes, try hard, do your best, keep agreements, and so on. But sooner or later, someone is going to point out the error in your ways. Often in subtle versions that still have an implicit criticism, such as giving advice, helping or teaching when you don't really need it, making corrections, or comparing you negatively to others.

In other words, criticism is unavoidable. We're not robots or big bugs, and it's natural for criticism to be uncomfortable, and sometimes hurt. But whatever sting is *inherent* in what is valid in the criticism, we add to this pain with the jabs we give ourselves. This "bonus pain"—a self-inflicted wound—includes repeating the criticism inside your head long after the other person has moved on. We also jab ourselves with needless pain when we brace ourselves against possible *future* criticism, or play small to avoid it. But much of the time, the criticism is never actually going to happen! We tend to transfer into adulthood expectations we acquired as children, or as younger adults. Maybe you did experience a great deal of criticism back then, but today you're probably with different—and hopefully less critical—people. Personally, I've spent way too much of my life hunkering down or overpreparing to preempt an anticipated shaming attack . . . that was, in truth, very unlikely.

And even if the criticism does come, will it actually be the terrible experience you dread? Usually not. You can roll with it, take what's useful, form your own conclusions about the person making the criticism, learn from it, and move on.

How

When criticism comes your way, pause and sort it out in your own mind so you're sure you understand it. It might be narrow and specific, but a lot of criticism is vague, confusing, or exaggerated. As you try to make sense of it, you can shore yourself up by thinking about people who care about you, and by remembering some of the many ways that you do good and are good.

Once you understand the criticism, you can decide for yourself what to do about it. Some criticisms of you will be flat-out mistaken, when the other person is wrong on the facts or doesn't understand the larger context. You have the right to disagree with them, if only inside your own mind.

Other criticisms will come from preferences or values that you just don't share. For example, some people want more closeness than others. Simply because you like more cave time than your partner (let's say) doesn't make you cold or rejecting. Nor is your partner being smothering or controlling. There is only a normal difference in values; talking about it with curiosity and compassion might be appropriate, but not with criticism.

There are also times when we do something that indeed calls for skillful correction—sometimes I *have* driven too fast, and my wife was right that I should slow down—but the criticism comes wrapped with emotional intensity, shaming, or personal attack. As we saw in chapter 11 ("Forgive Yourself"), it's very useful to separate what is indeed a moral fault from what is simply something to fix and learn from. You might choose to push back against the uncalled-for "wrapping" around whatever is actually valid about the criticism, or you might decide to ignore it and focus only on being more skillful in the future.

Sometimes we do things that are worthy of appropriate remorse. Make amends if you can, ask yourself how much remorse you'd want a friend to bear who did what you did, and then see if you can ask no more or less from yourself.

When you know you can handle criticism in these ways, it's not so upsetting, and you can let yourself be more open to it. You won't feel the need to be defensive, or to stonewall or counter-attack others who criticize you. You won't have to bend over backward to avoid trouble, or obsess or over-plan to make sure you make no mistakes.

Mostly, just recognize that criticism in its various forms and flavors is a fact of life. So be it. Our lives and this world have bigger problems, and much bigger opportunities. Time to live more confidently and bravely.

24

Take Care of Your Side of the Street

A fundamental idea in social psychology is that relationships typically develop a stable equilibrium that resists change, *even if they are full of conflict and suffering*. While doing couples counseling, I've seen versions of this many times. Each person has things they don't like about the relationship. Each one wishes that the other person would act differently in some ways. Each of them has a pretty good idea of what their partner would like. But they're stuck. Essentially, Partner A says to Partner B, "I'll change if you change," and B replies, "Sure! You first."

We tend to spend much more time thinking about how others could treat us better than we think about how to treat them better ourselves. This gets intensified when there's significant conflict. We become experts in what they could and should do better.

Of course, they have their list as well.

As normal as this is, it creates deadlocks, vicious cycles, and escalating spirals in our relationships. Things may seem hopeless. Emotionally, it's like marinating in a chronic sense of hurt and resentment.

The alternative is what I call *unilateral virtue*, which means living by your own code even when others don't. Sure, put 20 percent or so of your attention on what they could do better . . . and 80 percent on what you could do better yourself. Take maximum reasonable responsibility for addressing the wishes and grievances of the other person—knowing that *you* decide what "maximum reasonable responsibility" means.

At first you might think: *Grrrr, why should I go first? They've done me so wrong.* But there are many benefits in you taking care of your side of the street—as *you* judge best. Immediately, there is less sense of stuckness and helplessness because you're focusing on where you *do* have control—which is over yourself—rather than where you don't: the other person. No matter what another person does, it feels good to walk a higher road and enjoy the "bliss of blamelessness." Plus it's your best-odds strategy for being treated better by others, as you turn down the emotional heat, address their issues, and give them less to find fault with. Over time, this approach will put you in a stronger position to ask—and, if need be, insist—that they respond to your own needs and wants as well.

How

The essence of this is simple: focusing primarily on what *you* can do to improve the relationship. In life, we can "tend to the causes," but we cannot control the results. You can water a fruit tree, but you can't *make* it give you an apple. Shifting mentally from a preoccupation with others to your own checklist of things to do today can feel like a wonderful relief.

Find What's Authentic

This does not mean putting on a happy smile and acting like everything is OK if it's not. In any moment, there is a range of how we can authentically respond to another person, and unilateral virtue means aiming for the high end of that range. For example, if things have been tense with someone, you could stay civil while being cool, distant, and formal. At the same time, you would take care of your tasks and keep your agreements while staying out of dead-end struggles to get them to change.

Take Care of Yourself

To keep on the higher road, treat yourself well, including in the ways we discussed in part one. Beware the things that cloud your mind and lead to over-reactions, such as too little sleep or too much alcohol. Stay motivated by remembering the benefits to you and others.

Fulfill Your Responsibilities

On paper or in your mind, identify your responsibilities related to the relationship. Depending on the situation, they might include tangible items such as "do the dishes every other night; turn in the weekly sales report by 4 p.m. on Fridays." There could be more global or emotional items, such as "stay present in conversations; be supportive when we're interacting with the in-laws." Consider *relationship tasks*, such as "set aside 'us' time; ask questions about what they're feeling." You could imagine your "job description" as a parent, employee, adult child of an aging parent, spouse, friend, or simply a decent human being. While this might seem weirdly formal, putting it this way can make it feel more impersonal and thus simply what you ought to do, regardless of how well others fulfill their own responsibilities.

Live by Your Code

What's going to give you a feeling of self-respect when you go to sleep each day? This is your personal code of conduct. While it may already seem obvious, it's useful to make it explicit in your mind or on paper. It might include things like these: *Do give others equal time to speak; don't get high in front of the kids; stop harping on my points; be helpful when I can; keep my agreements.* Think back on times when you were caught up in conflicts: How do you wish you'd acted?

Address Their Complaints

Complaints are normal. Most of us have complaints about others. In relationships, the complaints of the other person are usually pretty clear, and you can ask if you're unsure. Knowing what's on their Complaint List—or, if you like, their Wish List—think about what you could *reasonably* do to take care of some, most, or even all of their items. Imagine what it would be like to gradually work through their list, and the benefits for you and the relationship.

Take the Higher Road

It's really good to know what *unilateral virtue* means to you. Then a lot of life becomes clearer: Just do your job—as *you* define it. It may not be easy, others may get in the way, and your situation might still be very challenging. Still, you can find a sense of peace and self-worth in simply walking your path each day.

As you do this, you'll see how others respond. After a reasonable amount of time—measured in weeks or months, not years—you can reassess the relationship and decide whether you want to talk more about your own wishes and complaints. If you do, it will be on a much stronger foundation. And, all the while, in your heart you'll know that you've done the best you could.

Part Four

Stand Up
for Yourself

25

Let Go of Needless Fear

It's normal to be cautious or nervous around other people. For example, if somebody disagrees with you in a meeting, you might feel uneasy and worried about what others think: *Was I too pushy? Does my boss like me? Do they think I'm not very smart?* When you get home later that day, let's say your teenage son is quiet and prickly, as usual. You want to tell him that the chilly distance between you feels awful, and you want to open your heart to him . . . but it feels awkward, you're afraid of making things worse, and when you spoke from the heart while growing up it did not go well, so you say nothing, again.

Other social anxieties include fears about your appearance, public speaking, talking with authority figures, or being around people who aren't like you. Sometimes these fears are justified. Someone might actually want to pressure, hurt, or exploit you. Safety is our most fundamental need, and it's vital to be clear-eyed about threats and skillful in dealing with them. Nonetheless, many of our fears around other people are not actually justified. They don't really care about what we did or, if they do, it's a passing feeling.

And if you're facing a genuine threat, you can be determined and confident without being anxious about it. Anxiety is something that's *added* to our responses. Sometimes it's helpful, but so often it clouds our thinking, compounds suffering, and worsens conflicts with others. We can have too little or too much anxiety around other people. Which is more common?

It's the second one: needless anxiety stirred into the sauce of life, making it bitter.

How

Anxiety can become chronic, a kind of habit, and hard to budge. People can even be anxious about not being anxious, since then they might lower their guard, and get hurt again. It's important to realize that *you can be alert and strong about potential threats while not feeling anxious.*

Be aware of the costs of unnecessary—not informative, not useful—anxiety. Besides feeling bad, it makes us play smaller with others, hold back what we really feel, and hunker down—or get combative. Decide in your heart if you want to be free of worthless fears.

Let Go of Paper Tiger Paranoia

It helps to understand why the nervous system is so easily hijacked by alarm. To keep our ancestors alive, Mother Nature developed a brain that tends to overestimate threats, underestimate opportunities, and underestimate resources to deal with threats and fulfill opportunities. This is good for survival in life-or-death conditions, but it's lousy for well-being and fulfilling relationships. It's not our fault that we're needlessly anxious. But it *is* our responsibility—and our *opportunity*—to address it.

So, whenever something seems threatening to you—such as what you think might happen if you were more vulnerable, emotional, or assertive with someone—ask yourself:

- Am I overestimating this threat?
- Am I underestimating the opportunities here?
- Am I underestimating the resources—both inside me and around me—for dealing with this threat and capitalizing on these opportunities?

This stepping back to understand your own mind can immediately help you feel less anxious.

Recognize Your Turbochargers

Consider the life that you've had, especially your childhood, and what has been threatening, scary, even traumatic about it. How have you learned to deal with threats and manage anxiety? These lessons might have been helpful at the time, but now they are lodged in the body like turbochargers, distorting your perceptions, speeding up and tilting your emotions, and driving your impulses and actions. Take a little time to make a list of your own "turbochargers." As you become more aware of them, they'll have less power over you. You can talk to yourself in wise ways like these: *This is not junior high school . . . He is not my dad . . . What they said was critical, but it was not a horrible attack . . . I have not been totally rejected, even though it feels like that . . . These hurt feelings are mainly old emotional memories, not based on what is true here and now.*

Don't Be Afraid

Bring to mind someone you *know* cares about you, and try saying to yourself: *I know you're not going to attack me.* Find your way to having the statement ring true, and then see how you feel. Do it again with this statement to yourself: *Even if you did attack me, I would still be OK in the core of my being.* Let the truth of this and related good feelings sink into you. Here's another one: *I can take care of myself when I am with you.* Let this, too, sink in. And: *If you hurt me, I'll still be OK in my core.* And: *I wish you well.* If you have any difficulty with this practice, try it with other people who love you. Draw on the sense of calm strength that we've previously explored. Try to feel your way into a place in which you recognize others and situations as they truly are, you take care of your own needs, and *no needless anxiety is added.*

Next, do this practice by bringing a friend to mind . . . and then do it with a neutral person . . . and then with someone who is challenging for you. If there is truly something to be anxious about, so be it. Otherwise, keep opening to the experience of being realistic about others and strong on your own behalf—without feeling any pointless fear.

Try this approach while actively interacting with others. Can you talk with a family member, a friend, a neutral person, and a challenging person without one bit of *unnecessary* worry, alarm, or uneasiness? As you deepen your sense of being appropriately fearless with others, keep letting this experience sink in so you become increasingly grounded in this way of being.

Enjoy the sense of freedom this practice brings, the greater ease with others, the confidence. Notice how you can be more relaxed, patient, open, and caring with other people when you are not afraid.

26

Find Your Ground

've been to New Zealand several times, and really respect and like it. I learned a Maori word there—*tūrangawaewae*, "a place to stand"—that's meant a lot to me over the years.

I'm sure I don't know the full meaning of the word in its cultural context. But at a basic level, it's clear that we all need a place to stand. A physical place, to be sure—hearth and home, land and sea, a bed to curl up in—but also psychological or spiritual places, such as feeling loved, a calm clear center inside, knowledge of the facts, compassion and ethics, and realistic plans. A related notion is that of *refuge*: those things that offer sanctuary, nurturance, and inspiration. For example, a person might find refuge in a trusted teacher, a body of wisdom, and a community of good-hearted people.

We need a place to stand, even in the best of circumstances. And challenges keep coming. Maybe your partner has just flared up at you or you've found out that a coworker has badmouthed you behind your back. Perhaps you're facing a health problem, financial trouble, or a global pandemic. Whenever you're shaken by anything, it's especially important to find and hold your ground.

How

Find Your Immediate Footing

Start with your body, and the simple, undeniable feeling of being *here*. The sensations of breathing . . . the feeling of your feet on the floor, your back against a chair. When you stand, you can bend your knees a little and feel centered and grounded. Notice that you are *going on being*—the groundbreaking pediatrician and psychoanalyst Donald Winnicott's term for the fundamental need, all the way back to infancy, to feel and to know that you *are*, that you're continuing. It seems so obvious, and yet it's deeply reassuring.

This sense of ongoing being helps you stay in the present. Whatever the past has been and whatever the future may hold, all that is true *now* is absolutely true in the present and cannot be taken from you. Try to separate thoughts and fears about the future from the reality of the present. What is true right now? Probably many good things. There is a trustworthy stability in awareness. Your mind is working, you can think and plan and function. Even if there is stress and sorrow, are you basically OK in the core of your being? Most of the time, most people are *basically alright right now*. Recognizing the fact of this, again and again, is so calming and such an antidote to anxiety; this is one of the most powerful practices I know.

Look around you. What is supportive and reliable? Physical objects, such as chairs and walls, forks and pencils, food and water. People near and far, friends and family, professionals in physical and mental health, teachers and other sources of wisdom. We get used to the good that endures and the brain tunes it out, so try to deliberately notice it, and then let that noticing become feelings of reassurance and confidence.

See Clearly

To find your ground, establish the relevant *facts*. Unless it's an emergency, buy yourself some time to be sure about what happened. For example, what did the other person actually say? In what context? With what tone and apparent intent? Were others involved, and in what ways? What are the ongoing factors that could lead to a repeat, such as someone thinking that they don't really have to keep their agreements with you?

Some people may not like your efforts to see clearly, to get to the bottom of things. There might be lots of reasons for this, from just not wanting to take the time to talk about it . . . to being defensive and not wanting to admit a mistake . . . to deliberate deceit. If the other person is used to being dominant in the relationship, it might get intense if you push back against their denials and distractions. Still, you can open your heart with compassion while closing your head to those who could be trying to get into it to confuse or intimidate you.

If the issue is not that important to you and you can tell that pushing for clarity is going to create a cost in your relationship that's just not worth it, then you can back off. On the other hand, you might decide that the other person's discomfort is not itself a big enough reason to be unclear about something that matters. For example, I've worked with various professionals, including plumbers, electricians, lawyers, and doctors. All of them were well-intended. Sometimes they'd say that something was true or a priority, and it wouldn't make sense to me, so I'd try to find out more. My wife might roll her eyes—and sometimes the professional as well. Nonetheless, I'd keep asking, politely. Most of the time, they'd clarify that I'd misunderstood in some way. But maybe one time in twenty, my questions would surface something important.

If you have a funny feeling about something, trust it. Yes, we often can't find out every last detail. But you can usually get a good idea about what happened and could happen again.

Make a Plan

Knowing what you're going to *do*, at least the next step, is calming and grounding. It could be simple and concrete, such as you're going to put a little calendar on the refrigerator for the things that you schedule as a couple. Or it might be more general and far-reaching, such as deciding to gradually disengage from a relationship.

The purpose of a plan is to achieve particular goals. With this person, in this relationship, what matters most to you? What are your priorities, your relevant values? What do you care about? What do you think is your duty to others, and to yourself? In effect: *What's your why?*

When you're trying to find your ground, it can help to think about:

- **Your personal practice**—How can you protect and strengthen your own well-being and functioning? This is the foundation of everything, plus it's what is most under your direct control. For example, you could commit to spending a little more time each day meditating, loving others, and giving thanks. This is a good plan! You could also decide to disengage from interactions, people, or media that add little value and feel stressful.
- **Protecting your own interests**—Are you in any immediate danger? It's a sad fact that domestic violence is commonplace in every sector of society. If you have been or might be abused physically or emotionally, the standard recommendation is to

talk with a professional about this before trying to address it with the other person. Or perhaps you're in an organization and dealing with a mediocre supervisor or an adversarial coworker; if so, your plan might include building a paper trail of your concerns and finding allies and mentors—and maybe looking for a better job elsewhere. Take a fresh look at your health, finances, and preparations for an emergency; it might seem overwhelming at first, but you can make a list of sensible actions and chip away at them one day at a time.

- **For the sake of others**—Perhaps a teacher just won't be responsive to your child's particular needs, so your plan might range from simply riding out the school year to trying to switch to another class. Or your mother has had a stroke and your plan is to find a higher level of at-home care for her.

In your planning and in the actions that follow, focus on what's within your control. Make a list and work through it. There's no replacement for effective action. In my experience as a therapist, many people know what they ought to do but just don't do it. Take a step, look around, and take another step. Keep going. Action eases anxiety.

Know that you are not alone. Whatever you're dealing with, from a tiff with a roommate to a worry about a child to a deep concern about your country, other people right now are also dealing with it or something similar. You care about people, and people care about you. We live in a web of relationships, even if it's tattered in some ways. You can feel a camaraderie with others who are also shaken and trying to find their own ground.

27

Use Anger;
Don't Let It Use You

A nger is tricky. On the one hand, anger—feeling irritated, resentful, fed up, mad, outraged, or enraged—alerts us to real threats, real injuries, and real wrongs that need correcting, and it energizes us to do something about them. In my family growing up, my parents had a monopoly on anger. So I suppressed my own, along with many other feelings, and it's been a long journey to reclaim my own interior, including the anger in it.

Whether in personal relationships or society in general, people with more power or privilege may tell others that they shouldn't get so worked up when, in fact, they have every reason and right to be angry. In any situation, you can form your own view about what is happening, how bad it is, and whether you want to get or stay angry.

On the other hand, anger:

- Feels bad past the first rush of it.
- Narrows our attention, so we lose sight of the big picture.
- Clouds our judgment, driving us to act impulsively, potentially violently.
- Creates and intensifies conflicts with others.

Anger can seem *so* justified if you feel attacked, wronged, let down, or provoked: *Of* course *I'm mad, you* made *me mad, it's* your *fault.* It's seductive, often coming with a rush of dopamine that feels rewarding. Nonetheless, it hurts the person who is angry. For example, chronic hostility poses a significant risk to physical health, including cardiovascular disease. In this metaphor from early Buddhism, "Anger has a honeyed tip, and a poisoned barb." Or consider the saying, "Resentment is like taking poison and waiting for others to die."

Anger hurts others, too, sometimes in ways that come back to hurt us. There are four major types of negative emotions—anger, fear, sadness, and shame—and it's anger that typically has the greatest impact on other people. You have to flare up only once at someone for them to permanently alter their relationship with you—as I've learned to my infinite regret. Two people can get caught in vicious cycles of grievance and payback. Similar processes happen in groups as well, from one family against another to entire nations. Groups often form a shared identity around shared grievances, and throughout history many leaders have exploited this to increase their own power.

So, how can you find that balance in which you respect and use your anger without being poisoned by it and without causing needless trouble in your relationships?

How

When we get angry, it often happens in two stages. First there is the *priming*, such as a growing sense of fatigue, hunger, pain, stress, frustration, hurt, or mistreatment. Then there is the *trigger*, perhaps someone making a thoughtless comment. The priming is like a pile of matches and the trigger is the spark that ignites a bonfire.

Take Care of the Priming

Try to be mindful of the priming and deal with it early on before it builds up. Inside yourself, you could take a big breath with a long exhalation, look out the window for a minute, get a snack, think of something that gives you a feeling of peace or love, or find a general sense of acceptance in which you may not like the way it is but you're not mad about it. Outside yourself, you could do what you can to improve your situation, such as turning off a TV news show that's starting to really bug you or ending an exasperating phone call. Longer term, you could use the ideas and tools in part five of this book to address issues in your relationships.

Slow It Down

When triggers land, try to slow down before you say or do anything you'll regret later. In your brain, incoming information—perhaps a car cutting you off on the highway or a dismissive word from your partner—is processed along two tracks (to summarize complex processes). The first track runs quickly through subcortical regions, such as the amygdala, which can launch the neurohormonal stress response in less than a second. Now your heart is beating faster, adrenaline and cortisol are starting to surge through your bloodstream, and feelings of fear and anger are boiling up in your mind. Along the second track, your prefrontal regions are beginning to come online to figure out what happened, how big a deal it is, and what to do about it. The prefrontal cortex (PFC) is a fantastic piece of biological equipment, but it's slow compared to the subcortex, which has a head start in driving your impulses.

When you pause for even a few seconds to gather yourself, your PFC can catch up and bring in a sense of the big picture, your long-term interests, the needs of others, different options, and a step-by-step action plan.

Listen to the Anger

Whether your anger comes in a burst or it's more of an underlying mood of irritation and aggravation, it's telling you something important. You can be prudent in how you express it while still opening to it inside yourself and exploring it.

What does it feel like in your body? What kind of thoughts come with it about other people? What sense of self does it bring, such as being put-upon or mistreated? Is there a history to this anger, perhaps in a particular relationship or more generally in your life, such as many experiences of being pushed around in your childhood or being discriminated against as an adult? What desires are there, such as to withdraw or lash out?

Is there anything underneath the anger? There might be softer, perhaps younger feelings, such as frustration, hurt, worry, guilt, or defeat. Is anger a way to keep pushing down these more vulnerable feelings?

Is there a message in the anger that's important for you to hear? For example, are you getting stretched too thin, so that you need to dial back or others need to step up—or both? Have things gone too far with someone and you need to clear the air? Is someone inadvertently annoying you because they don't know any better, and they'd stop it if you told them? Are you mad at *yourself* about something and taking it out on others? Do you keep having interactions with someone in which you feel misunderstood or disrespected, and it's time to make a change in that relationship?

As silly as it might seem, in your mind you could ask the anger what it is trying to tell you; you might be surprised at what it says.

In the middle of an argument or an upsetting experience, it may be very helpful to tune into yourself in these ways. Outside the heat of the moment, you could take some time to consider the questions just above if there is a recurring issue in a relationship or it's challenging in general. If others minimize, invalidate, or criticize your feelings of anger, try to find out why they're doing that. Is it well-intended, even if possibly misguided, or are they doing it out of their own self-interest?

Don't Let Anger Drive the Bus

Some years ago I made a personal commitment not to speak or act *from* anger. I doubt anyone would have described me as an angry person, yet that commitment made me realize how often anger was motivating and infusing what I said and did, even mildly through eye rolls, tone of voice, exasperated sighs, critical words, or bossy instructions. You might ask yourself how often anger "leaks" out of you. There might be certain situations in which you feel that acting from anger is necessary and appropriate, such as fighting for your life, confronting injustice, or energizing yourself to break out of an abusive relationship. But in general, you can be true to yourself while not speaking or acting from anger. You can feel it and listen to it, and tap into its energy and focus, without letting it control you.

Depending on the situation, you might stay quiet, be watchful, and bide your time until a more appropriate moment comes along. Or you might speak firmly, assertively, even intensely. You could say that you are angry about something without pouring that anger onto others. You could take a break in a conversation if you're getting riled up. You could acknowledge your feelings of anger, and then talk about what is underneath them, such as feeling misunderstood or let down.

As I did, you will likely find that this commitment puts you on a stronger footing with others. You'll be better able to talk about the fundamental matters that lie beneath the anger. Other people won't be so likely to divert attention from *what* you are saying because of *how* you're saying it. Think of people who are models for you of strength and effectiveness without being hostile or hateful, and get a sense of what it would be like to be more this way yourself.

A proverb tells us that acting from anger is like throwing hot coals with bare hands; both people get burned. There has been so much burning already in our shared human history. Too much burning. Too many minds burned up with anger.

Honesty, advocacy, fierce compassion, setting a boundary, confronting wrongdoing, protecting others—none of these is itself anger or requires anger. Truly, we can speak from the heart with the power of a self-respect and a courage that is free of anger.

28

Tell the Truth and Play Fair

L ike many people, I worry sometimes about what it will take for all of us to live together in peace—whether in a couple or family, in a community or country, or in the world as a whole. Then I remember what I heard in school: *Tell the truth. Play fair.*

This is what we ask our own kids to do. It's what we look for in a friend, a boss, and a neighbor. If your child doesn't know any better and tries to cheat on a board game, you point it out; it's not OK. We want cashiers to give us the correct change and mechanics to be honest about the repairs a car needs. It's basic. These principles might seem abstract, but when you think about common, everyday situations—a coworker who smiles to your face but trashes you behind your back, a romantic partner who is unfaithful, a boss who won't acknowledge your contributions—you can see how relevant they are.

People have disagreements, and sometimes they compete with each other. Conflicts are a normal part of just about any relationship. But whether it's a game of cards, two parents arguing about how to share housework, or candidates trying to win an election, we expect a level playing field. Rights for them are also rights for us, and rules for us are also rules for them. If everyone accepts these standards, winning is all the sweeter because you earned it. Losing may be bitter, but at least you know you weren't cheated.

Good process leads to good results. So if there are bad results—from bullying on a playground to a nation in trouble—it makes sense to figure out the bad process that led to those results. In relationships of all kinds, good process must include telling the truth and playing fair. It is not a guarantee, but lying and cheating *are* guaranteed to poison any kind of relationship over time.

How

We start with our own side of the street. We may get heated, argumentative, even over-the-top, but there's no lying. If we get some facts wrong, we admit it—at least eventually. We don't punish people for trying to find the truth. We don't speak in bad faith, counterattack, or get provocative to muddy the waters. If we say something is bad for others to do, we try not to do it ourselves. This doesn't mean being some kind of saint. It's just calling ourselves to the basic standards we'd want in any school classroom.

But then what can you do with those who won't do the same?

See What You See

Tell the truth to *yourself* about what is happening. It may be shocking (and hard to believe) that somebody doesn't really feel the need to be honest or fair with you—especially if they've been likable in other ways. Watch over time and see whether they are being deliberately dishonest or just wrong about the facts. Are they truly narcissistic or even sociopathic—or simply preoccupied or socially clueless? Do they regard you as only a means to their ends, not as a being who matters in your own right?

Ordinary exaggerations, sales pitches, rants, snark, and pushiness are one thing, but repeated lying and cheating is another. *The disregard for truth-telling and fair play is the fundamental issue.* Recognizing this when it is happening is so clarifying. You may be unable to change anything out in the world, but at least inside your mind you can stand on solid ground.

Find Allies

We all need allies. Consider whom you could draw on to see what is happening and perhaps help you with it. For example, in various situations, I have reached out to friends, family members, colleagues, mentors, lawyers, and state regulatory agencies.

And others need us to be allies with them as well.

Speak Out

Lying and cheating, in one form or another, are a kind of "freeloading," in which one person takes advantage of others. Throughout most of our history, people have lived in small bands or villages in which they could come together to identify, shame, and punish freeloaders. *Shame* and *punish* are strong words. But without them, there would have been no consequences for freeloading, and our hominid and human ancestors would not have been able to evolve our magnificent capacities for cooperation, generosity, and justice.

Sometimes it is not safe to call out a freeloader, such as a bully, a con artist, a casual liar, or a sexual predator. Then you protect yourself and others as best you can.

But if you *can* do it, shine a bright light on violations of truthtelling and fair play, ideally with allies who do the same. Liars and cheaters are usually good at distracting others with wild and dramatic counterclaims. So we need to stay focused on the fundamental values of honesty and fairness, and not get bamboozled by side issues. Keep coming back to simple, powerful questions like these: *Why do you keep lying? Why do you need to cheat to win? Are you trustworthy? Why should anyone ever listen to you again?*

Recognize the Political Level

I'm a psychologist and focus mainly on the level of individuals. Still, many of the forces that hurt us personally come from the *political* level. Honest and honorable people may have intense disagreements about how to run a village or a country. But we can find common ground in the basic principles of no lying and no cheating—and may the best team win. This is what we need to come together about. The central political issue of our time is not between the left and the right. It is between those who will tell the truth and play fair—and those who will not.

Lying is a firing offense in any business and should be the same in any elected office. We can flag liars on Twitter while staying out of stupid arguments. We can support journalists, scientists, and lawyers who get to the truth of things. We can focus on the foundation of any democracy: having elections that are free and fair and inclusive. If people have to lie and cheat to get into and then hold onto high office, they may have legal authority but they will never have moral legitimacy.

Anyone, high or low, who lies and cheats—and anyone who supports such people—would lose all standing in a schoolyard, church or temple, marketplace, or village commons. We need exactly the same to happen in our own public square. Because we all live in this square, and what happens there has very personal consequences for each one of us.

29

Don't Be Bullied

Power is an inherent aspect of most of our relationships. In any hierarchy, the person who is one-up has more power than the person who is one-down. Some people have appropriate authority over others, such as a teacher over students in a classroom. Power is not inherently good or bad. The question is, *how* do we use it? If we have power over people, we have responsibilities to them. We can use our power for good purposes, pursued in good ways.

Reflect for a moment about power in your relationships. Who tends to be more dominant, who tends to get the last word or make the final call? Who has higher status? Who is presumed to be better informed, smarter, more competent, or psychologically healthier? In a key relationship, do you feel that you ought to be more assertive, perhaps about particular things? Or is there an intuition that you should make more room for the other person? This exploration can be *very* illuminating.

Relationships can have an ordinary rough-and-tumble. Maybe somebody is too bossy, too controlling, too pushy. Not great, but common . . . and eventually others might push back.

And then there are *abuses* of power. These come in many forms, including the mistreatment of vulnerable people, physical or emotional intimidation, criminal fraud, structural discrimination, and tyranny. As an umbrella term, I'll use a simple down-to-earth word for this: *bullying*.

Unfortunately, bullies are common. In our homes, schoolyards, organizations, and politics, they create enormous suffering. What can we do about that?

How

Recognize Bullies

Bullies are:

- **Dominating**—Have to be the alpha; look for targets who seem weaker; lack compassion.
- **Defensive**—Don't admit fault; scorn others; avoid responsibility.
- **Deceptive**—Manipulate grievances to gain support; cheat; hide the truth since their power is based on lies.

Try to be aware of any innocence or naivete inside you that just can't believe another person or group would act that way. As the writer and activist Maya Angelou put it: *When someone shows you who they are, believe them the first time.*

Recognize Enablers

Some individuals and organizations tolerate or even value bullies, such as cheering on someone who is hurting people that they look down on. This enabling takes different forms, including pretending that all is normal or claiming falsely that "Both sides do it." From playgrounds to parliaments, people with an "authoritarian personality style"—dominance oriented and harshly punitive—have an affinity for leaders who are bullies, and usually form the core of their supporters.

Protect Yourself

Sometimes you are stuck with a bully, at least for a while. Be careful. Weigh your options and do what's best for you and those you care about.

Have Compassion

Deep down, the mind of a bully is like a hell realm of fended-off feelings of weakness and shame, always threatening to invade. Lots of suffering there. Compassion for a bully is not approval. It can be calming and strengthening for *you*.

And certainly the targets of bullies deserve our care. Even if you can do nothing to help them, your compassion is still authentic. It matters to *you*, and it may matter to others in ways you'll never know.

Name It

Tell the truth to yourself. Tell it to others.

And, if appropriate, tell the truth to bullies and their enablers. This might be a version of that truth: *You are a bully. You cheated and lied to get your power. You act tough but you're actually weak and frightened. You might be able to harm me and others, but I am not afraid of you. I see what you are.*

Bullies know that their power is on thin ice. Try to name the lying, the cheating, the weakness. Name the fakery, name the illegitimacy.

Stand with Others

Bullies target lone individuals and vulnerable groups to display dominance and create fear—which has been called "performative cruelty." So try to find allies who will stand with you if you're being bullied. For example, if you're being hassled (or worse) by a co-worker, you could tell friends about it and get their support, and then talk with your supervisor or the human resources department, if your company has one. You can ask others to stand up to bullies; sitting on the sidelines just perpetuates bullying.

Together, we can stand with and for people in general who have been or are being bullied. It may make no material difference. But it always makes a moral and psychological difference to those who stand up—and to those they stand up for.

Punish Bullying

I mean *punish* in the sense of justice, not vengeance. The act of bullying itself is rewarding to a bully, even if there's no concrete benefit. It's like pulling a pleasurable lever on a slot machine that sometimes delivers a jackpot: If you're a bully, why not keep pulling?

So there must be a real cost—and in terms the bully cares about. Hand-wringing and expressions of concern are irrelevant to a bully. Enablers also need to pay a price. Otherwise, why would they stop?

Since bullying is common, people have developed a variety of ways to punish it. Depending on the situation, you could:

- With moral confidence, name the bullying for what it is.
- Dispute false claims of legitimacy.
- Laugh at bullies (who are usually thin-skinned).

- Confront lies, including denial of harms they're doing.
- Build up sources of power to challenge the bully.
- Confront enablers; they're complicit in the bullying.
- Engage the legal system.
- Remove bullies from positions of power.

See the Big Picture

Bullying is enabled and fostered by underlying conditions. Bullies sometimes draw power from the grievances of others; when we address those grievances, we can reduce the bully's power.

Bullies try to dominate our attention much as they try to dominate everything else. But there is a larger world beyond their control. It contains so many things that are working, enjoyable, beautiful, and virtuous. Disengage as much as possible from ruminating on helpless outrage, fantasies of payback, and finding fault with others "who aren't doing enough." Bad enough that the bully is out there in the world. Try not to let the bully invade your own mind.

Part Five

Speak Wisely

30

Watch Your Words

As kids we used to chant: *Sticks and stones can break my bones, yet words will never hurt me.* But that's not actually true. What we say—and the tone that comes with it—can cause real damage. Just think back to things said to you over the years—especially with anger, rejection, or scorn—and the impacts they've had on you.

Words can literally hurt, since the emotional pain networks in your brain overlap with physical pain networks. The effects can linger—even for a lifetime, as the residues of hurtful words sift down into emotional memory and the inner landscape of your mind. Plus they can alter a relationship forever. Consider the ripple effects of things said between parents and children, from one sibling to another, among in-laws, or between friends.

Watching your words doesn't mean muzzling yourself, or getting fussy and rigid about particular ways of talking. It's simply a matter of being thoughtful and skillful, and keeping your highest values and long-term goals in mind. Clear guidelines are very useful, and that's what I'll focus on here.

How

I've been really helped by six principles offered in early Buddhism, and you'll recognize their essence in other traditions or philosophies. Wise speech is always:

1. **Well-intended**—It comes from goodwill, not ill will; it's constructive, not destructive, and tries to help rather than hurt.
2. **True**—It is factually accurate; you may not say everything that's true, but what you do say is indeed true, and not overstated or taken out of context.
3. **Beneficial**—It supports the happiness and welfare of yourself and others.
4. **Timely**—It comes at an appropriate time and has a good chance of being truly heard.
5. **Not harsh**—It could be firm, pointed, or intense; it could confront mistreatment or injustice; anger might be acknowledged, but it is not prosecutorial, nasty, inflammatory, dismissive, or disdainful.

And, if possible, it is:

6. **Wanted by the other person**—If they don't want to hear it, you may sometimes decide not to say it; but there will be other cases when you choose to speak up whether the other person likes it or not—and then it's more likely to go well if you follow the guidelines above.

There is certainly a place for talking loosely with others when it's comfortable to do so. And, realistically, in the first moments of an argument, sometimes people stray out of bounds.

But in important, tricky, or delicate interactions—or as soon as you realize you've gone over the line—it's time to communicate with care, and with wisdom. The six guidelines do not guarantee that the other person will respond the way you want. But they will raise the odds of a good outcome, plus you will know in your heart that you stayed in control of yourself, had good intentions, and have nothing to feel guilty about later.

You could reflect on these guidelines as you consider how to approach an important conversation. Then, be natural: If you're sincere, mean well, and keep returning to the truth as you know it, it is hard *not* to speak wisely! If things get heated, try to remember that how you speak is your own responsibility, no matter what the other person does. If you stray from the guidelines, acknowledge that to yourself and perhaps to the other person, and then return to them.

With time and a little practice, you will find yourself "speaking wisely" without consciously thinking about it. You might be amazed at the powerful, assertive ways you can communicate within the frame of the guidelines here.

And—as a bonus—how about practicing wise speech in the ways you talk to *yourself*?

31

Say What's True

When we say what's true, and say it clearly and appropriately, we feel good about ourselves. There's an honesty and
realness in the words that others can trust. But if we speak falsely,
distort what someone else has said, or present a false face, then
there are different results, such as unnecessary conflicts, lost opportunities to deepen a relationship, or a hollow, sad feeling in the
pit of the stomach.

The most important person to tell the truth to is yourself.
Many people don't speak truly to themselves in two ways: They
exaggerate their flaws and downplay their strengths. Further, if
you tell yourself that something is true but deep down you know
that it's not—such as "everything's fine" in a marriage that's actually cool and distant—you're living on thin ice. It's hard to build a
good life on that foundation.

Truth is bedrock. Even if you wish the truth were different, it's
what you can count on in a world that's full of spin, sales pitches,
disinformation, and plain BS. It's your refuge.

How

Speaking truly does not mean saying everything. You could cut
to the chase in a conversation, not burden children with more
than they can understand, and not spill your guts in a business

meeting. We don't have to confide more than is appropriate. I spent my twenties in a personal growth culture in which we said everything to everyone all the time—including the deepest, weirdest, wildest stuff. For a bottled-up person like me, popping this cork was valuable. But after a while, I learned that just because I *could* say something didn't mean I *should* say it. Some thoughts and feelings could be needlessly hurtful to others, or easily misunderstood, or used against you later on. Once it's out of your mouth—or released into cyberspace—there's no getting it back.

Being Authentic

But this does mean being genuine, honest, and real. Then your outer expression—tone, posture, facial expressions, and choice of words—is consistent with your inner experience. When I was learning how to open up, this was hard for me. I was being honest, but it sounded like I was reading a phone book. If you're feeling sad, hurt, anxious, or angry, are you able to feel it while you say it? Is there a particular emotion that's especially hard to stay in touch with? Or a particular desire, such as a longing to be included or appreciated? Slow it down when you're talking, give your feelings time to catch up to your words, and try to stay in touch with a feeling as you express it.

It's OK not to know exactly how to describe how you feel. Sometimes it's hard to find the words—or there just *aren't* any words. Nonetheless, your face and body can communicate so much.

Over time, you'll find that you can reveal more and more of yourself. Most of us have things that are hard to show to others.

For me growing up, it was feeling inadequate. For someone else, it might be fear or weakness; for another person, it might be anger. Perhaps something happened to you—or perhaps you did something yourself—that you've never told anyone about. Some people feel like they are living a kind of lie that's eating away at them. Is there anything that you've kept tucked out of sight that would be good to bring into the light? And could you deliberately talk about it with an appropriate person, even a therapist or a clergyperson, who's sworn to confidentiality? When it's finally out in the open, there's usually a sense of relief and a feeling of being more integrated and whole as a person.

What's Left Out?

In any relationship, ask yourself: *What's important that's not getting named? What's left out?* This applies both to you and to others. Consider the hurt or anxiety beneath irritation, or the rights or needs that are the real stakes in a seemingly silly quarrel. Is there an elephant in the room that no one is mentioning? Maybe someone has a problem with anger or with drinking too much, or is simply depressed. Maybe someone's high-powered job—sixty, seventy hours a week or more, counting commute and weekend emails—is crowding family life out to the margins. Our relationships are constrained by what we can't talk about. As you judge best, you have the right to bring topics to the table. And if other people keep trying to change the subject, you can highlight *that* fact as a topic you'd like to talk about.

Delivering Undelivered Communications

Depending on the relationship, speaking truly may mean expressing some of your undelivered communications to that other person. These are relevant and important things that you haven't said, maybe for good reasons at the time. Some undelivered communications fade away and don't matter. Others could continue to be significant for you, but it's still clear to you that they're better left unsaid. The pile that remains—however big it is—burdens and constrains a relationship as you (and sometimes the other person) maneuver around it.

In later chapters we'll explore *how* to express what's been unsaid in skillful ways. Here, I suggest that you take a little time to consider *what* you may have been holding back in key relationships. For a particular person, you could get out a sheet of paper, title it with something like "Undelivered Communications" or "Things I Haven't Told You," and then put down whatever comes to mind. Remember that you don't have to tell them anything that's on this page; this is your own exploration. As a prompt, you could imagine completing this sentence again and again: *I haven't told you* _____ . Be open to whatever you discover inside yourself. It might include times you felt let down and angry, or vulnerable intimate desires, or appreciation and lovingness. As you listen to the deeper layers of yourself, you may find that you actually have already said everything that matters—and you can enjoy this and be reassured by it. Try this exercise with a few people. Just getting it out onto the page can feel very freeing. And then, if you want, you can tell the other person when the time is right. Identifying your significant undelivered communications and then gradually expressing them in appropriate ways is one of the most powerful personal growth methods I know.

Last, accept the fact that no one is a perfect communicator. You're always going to leave something out, and that's OK. You have to give conversations room to breathe, without continually judging yourself as to whether you're speaking truly! Communicating is repairing. As long as you speak with basic sincerity and goodwill, your words will weave and mend a tapestry of truth in all your relationships.

32

Speak from the Heart

One Christmas I hiked down into the Grand Canyon, whose bottom lay a vertical mile below the rim. Its walls were layered like a cake, and stripes of red or gray rock revealed millions of years of erosion by the Colorado River. Think of water—so soft and gentle—gradually carving through the hardest stone to reveal great beauty. Sometimes what seems weakest is actually what's most powerful.

In the same way, speaking from an open heart can seem so vulnerable yet be the strongest move of all. Naming the truth—in particular, the facts of your experience, which no one can disprove—with simplicity and directness, has great moral force.

I remember a client of mine, a man whose marriage was smothered by the weight of so much unsaid. It was all normal-range things—like wishing his wife were less irritable with their children and more affectionate with him—but he feared that if he said any bit of it, that would be the end of their marriage. But *not* talking was what was actually crushing their relationship, with a mounting pile of hurts and resentments. Like two people on separate little icebergs, they were drifting apart in a frozen silence. Eventually, they divorced.

If you are addressing an issue in a relationship, speaking from your heart is compelling and usually moves others toward greater openheartedness themselves. And if it doesn't, the contrast between you and them is a powerful statement all by itself.

How

Speaking from the heart may feel scary. If you're just beginning to get used to this way of communicating, pick a topic, a person, and a moment that's likely to go well.

Before You Talk

Ground yourself in good intentions, such as to discover and express the truth, and to help yourself and the other person. Then get a basic sense of what you want to say. Focus on your *experience*: your thoughts, feelings, body sensations, wants, and anything else flowing through awareness. It's hard to argue with your experience, but easy to get into wrangles about situations, events, the past, or problem solving.

Try to find a sense of confidence inside. Have faith in your sincerity, and in the truth itself. Recognize that others may not like what you have to say, but you have a right to say it without needing to justify it. Know that the process of speaking from the heart is usually good for a relationship, even if what is said is difficult for the other person to hear.

When You Speak

Take a breath and settle into your body. It might help to get a quick sense of people who care about you. Soften your throat, eyes, chest, and heart. Try to find goodwill, even compassion, for the other person. Bring to mind what you want to say. Take another breath and start speaking.

Try to stay in touch with your experience as you express it, and minimize any persuasion or problem solving. (That's for later, if at all; see chapters 43–45.) Keep coming back to the essential point for *you*, whatever that is (especially if the other person gets reactive or tries to change the subject). And allow other aspects or deeper layers of what's in your heart to come forward as you speak. You don't need to know everything you are going to say before you start speaking.

Feel free to disengage if the other person is just not ready to hear you; maybe another time would be better. The primary purpose here is not to get the other person to change—which may or may not happen—but to express yourself in an openhearted way. As appropriate, you could ask the other person to speak from the heart as well.

Afterward, you can know that you did your best. It's brave and it's hard (especially at first) to speak from the heart. But so necessary in relationships of any depth.

33

Ask Questions

Asking questions brings you lots of important information and shows others that you're paying attention. It gives them the feeling that you are interested, that you care, that the topic on the table matters to you, and that *they* matter as well. It gets things out into the open for you and others to see. Asking questions can slow down heated conversations so they don't get out of hand. It gives you time to think, and prevents you from jumping to conclusions and making mistakes you'll regret. The other person may not always like your questions—perhaps you're clarifying that they dropped the ball, not you—yet you have the right to ask them.

In a deep way, asking questions gives you a portal into the vast mysterious interior of another person. What in the world is going on in there? Bubbling passions, soft wistful longings, memories and fantasies, a chorus of voices, layers and depths, and all of it swirling and surging along. Fascinating in its own right. And as we come to know others better, we can better know ourselves.

How

As a therapist, I ask questions for a living. Plus I've been married a long time through thick and thin, and raised two kids. As they say in medicine: Good judgment comes from experience . . . and experience comes from bad judgment. So I offer some lessons from my experiences!

Have Good Intentions

We don't have to ask questions like a prosecutor. You could be trying to get to the bottom of things, such as what your son will actually be doing this Saturday night or what your role is supposed to be in an upcoming business meeting. But try not to use questions to make others look bad.

Keep the Tone Gentle

Being asked a question—particularly, a series of questions—may feel invasive, critical, or controlling to the person on the receiving end. Think of all the times that kids get asked questions as a prelude to a scolding or another punishment. You could check in with the other person to make sure your questions are welcome. Slow questions down so they don't come rat-a-tat-tat. Try interspersing them with self-disclosure that matches, more or less, the emotional depth of what the other person is saying; this way they're not putting all their cards on the table while you keep yours close to the chest.

Stay Interested

You can tell when someone's attention wanders when you're speaking, and they will notice the same thing about you. Try to stay over there with *them*, rather than shifting your focus to a text that just came in on your phone or to what you plan to say next.

Try a sense of "beginner's mind," "don't-know mind," in which you're curious, open, and patient. What would you like to know more about? Try to find what's alive, fresh, juicy, meaningful, useful, or deep in the conversation. A raised eyebrow, a nod to say more, or simply letting there be a bit of silence are all signals to the other person to keep going.

Keep Asking

If you sense that there's still some problematic cloudiness in the other person's answers, or simply more to learn, you could ask a question again, maybe in a different way. Or explain—without accusation—why you're still unclear about what the other person is saying. It's startling how often people don't actually answer the question they've been asked. You might ask additional questions that could help pin down a key fact or uncover the deeper layers of the other person's thoughts, feelings, and intentions.

Inquire to Resolve an Issue

Questions about facts or plans are usually pretty straightforward. For the murkier and often emotionally charged territory of another person's inner world, here are some possibilities:

How was _____ for you? What are you feeling about _____?

What do you appreciate about _____? What do you think went well? Was anything reassuring? What did you like about _____?

What bothers [or worries] you about _____? What is it that you feel anxious [or frustrated, sad, hurt, angry, etc.] about? Are there other things you're feeling [or wanting] besides _____?

What did this remind you of? What's the context [or history] that matters to you here [for instance, past upsets between the two of us, being yet again overlooked for a promotion]?

What did you wish had happened instead? What's the most important thing here, for you?

How do you feel about me? What do you like about me? What do you, ah, not like about me? What do you wish I'd said or done? If there are one or two key things you think I should be handling, what are they?

What would it look like if you got what you wanted here? What would it look like if you got what you wanted from me? How would you like it to be from now on?

What else? Could you say more about _____?

Deepen an Intimate Friendship

Over time, a romantic relationship can be OK but a little humdrum, distant, even stale. A good way to enliven it is to learn new things about the other person, and here are some sample questions (you may know some of the answers already about your partner). You're not trying to play therapist—you're simply an interested friend—and you can dial the depth up or down as it feels right. If you like, you could suggest taking turns asking each other some of these questions. And, of course, add some of your own!

What's your earliest memory?

Did you have a favorite relative when you were young? What did you do with them?

As a kid, what did you imagine or think about as you fell asleep? How about these days?

When you were young, what did you really love doing? Any special memories? These days, what are your favorite things to do on your own? With me?

As a kid, did you have any favorite pets?

What was your first kiss? How did it go?!

What was it like to leave home? Were you eager to go? Or?

What do you think have been the big turning points in your life?

What do you like to think about or imagine?

If you could be any of the characters in the Lord of the Rings stories [or other well-known fiction], which one would you pick? Why?

If you lived twenty thousand years ago in a hunter-gatherer band, what role(s) would you naturally gravitate to?

If you could get a billion people to spend five minutes a day doing a particular thing, what would it be?

One way to explore these questions is to look at pictures together from your childhoods, and perhaps your adulthoods as well. When you look at the faces of the people in the pictures, you can imagine some of what life was like for them, which could lead to more good questions.

With your partner, you could do a kind of exercise in which you ask the same question over and over again, and then switch roles. Potential questions include: *What do you like about me? What do you want in our relationship? What do you need to trust me? In the days to come, what do you hope for yourself?* If you are answering the question, say what comes into your mind unless you think it would be really hurtful or reveal something you're just not yet ready to talk about. Notice if you are editing your answers, and see if it would be OK to more fully express yourself. If you are asking the question, accept whatever the other person says, say thank you, and ask the question again. It's OK to ask them to clarify something briefly, and then keep repeating the question. If they say something you'd like to pursue further, just make a mental note and you can come back to it later. This process can quickly get very deep. At a certain point, perhaps after a dozen or so rounds with the same question, there could be nothing new to say; it will feel complete, at least for now, and you can switch roles or try another question.

Summing up, it's really OK to ask questions. Usually, people welcome them. You can trust your good intentions and your good heart.

34

Express Appreciation

One of the most powerful ways to improve your relationships is also one of the simplest: Tell people what you appreciate about them. This is not flattery or manipulation. It has to come in good faith and be what you think is really true. You could say it to give thanks, offer support, or convey your respect. Hopefully, they appreciate your appreciation. But even if they brush it off for some reason, you can know that you were sincere.

When people achieve a goal, show good character, or simply keep going under tough conditions, it's appropriate to recognize that. We're social animals, and we need to feel seen and valued. If you're doing a good job at work or at home and nobody ever says anything about it, after a while it usually feels weird or worse.

Think about several people you care about. *What are some of their good qualities? Are they decent and honorable? Have they helped or contributed to you in any ways? If you were to write them letters of recommendation, what would you say?* Then ask yourself: *Of all the ways I could acknowledge these people, how many of them have I actually said?* You might already be expressing a lot of appreciation in your relationships—but, if so, that's pretty unusual in my experience. Much of the time we just don't think to acknowledge others, or it feels a little awkward, or we withhold appreciation as part of a larger conflict. It's all too easy to take others for granted, or drift into a mood of complaint about them.

Recall a time when someone really thanked you, praised your

work, acknowledged your efforts, or talked about good deep qualities inside you. It probably meant a lot to you, and it may have strengthened your relationship. You can have the same kind of beneficial effects on others when you tell them what you appreciate about them.

How

We appreciate others in two broad ways—through gratitude and praise.

Pick someone you care about and consider what you're thankful for, such as things they do that benefit you, standing up for you with others, or simply being warm and kind. You could be thankful for little things, like washing your coffee cup at work, or big ones, like raising children together. Notice how it feels to be grateful to this person.

Next, consider what's praiseworthy. What do you admire, honor, or respect about them? What are their talents and skills? Positive character traits? Inner strengths? What have they accomplished? What have they had to cope with? Are they funny, creative, soulful? Do they care about others? Are they doing things to help the world? What do you like about them? What dear, innermost qualities do you cherish in them? What does it feel like to recognize all this about that person?

Reflecting on this relationship, is there anything that feels under-acknowledged? What do you think they'd really like to hear? Perhaps this person is a child, or someone who really looks up to you. What could make a big difference to them?

Then ask yourself how you could express your gratitude and praise more fully. Imagine what you would actually say, and how and when. It's fine that people have different styles for conveying appreciation, and different ways they like to receive it. Imagine what the benefits might be for you and the other person and your relationship.

Notice any reluctance to express appreciation. It may feel at odds with how people talked in your family, or the norms in your culture. You might feel that it makes you vulnerable or dependent, or that the other person will now be one-up and have a claim on you, or that your valid complaints about them will be neutralized and have no standing. Or that it will encourage the other person to ask for more and more from you, as if they were a kind of needy vampire, sucking you dry. Try to step back from these various reasons, and ask yourself if they're really true. For example, you can recognize the value you get from others while being a strong and self-reliant person. You can appreciate the good ideas of a co-worker while prodding them to turn in their work on time. You can compliment someone who's intensely hungry for praise while setting boundaries in the relationship; you can recognize that feeding them does not need to deplete *you*.

Now pick a challenging relationship, perhaps one fraught with serious conflicts. With this person, is there anything you're grateful for about them? It's OK if there isn't anything—but if there is, try to recognize it. Consider what could be praised about them, even if it's alongside some major faults. How might you be able to say some of this to them? Perhaps a simple factual statement in passing that is hard to argue with. How might appreciating this person improve your relationship?

When you look for what you value in others, this usually helps you feel better about your world. It also puts things that bother you about someone in a larger context, so they're less upsetting, plus often now easier to talk about.

35

Try a Softer Tone

I remember times I felt frazzled or aggravated and then said something with an edge to it that just wasn't necessary or useful. Sometimes it was the words themselves—absolutes like *never* or *always*, or over-the-top phrases like *That was dumb*. More often it was the intonation in my voice, a harsh vibe or look, an abrupt way of speaking, or a put-upon air.

Linguists like Deborah Tannen have pointed out that most communications have three elements:

- **Explicit content**—"There is no milk in the refrigerator."
- **Emotional subtext**—Might be neutral, positive, or negative.
- **Implicit statement about the nature of the relationship**—Does one person get to criticize or boss around someone else? Is someone one-up, as-good-as, or one-down?

The second and third elements—which is what I mean by *tone*—usually have the greatest impact on how an interaction turns out, and over time the accumulating weight of the tone we use has big effects. A repeatedly critical, superior, disappointed, disdainful, or reproachful tone can really rock a relationship. For example, John and Julie Gottman's research has shown that it typically takes several positive interactions to make up for a single negative one. Apart from the effects on the relationship, there is the direct impact on the other person. A needlessly negative tone creates unnecessary suffering in others.

Becoming more mindful of your tone will put you more in touch with yourself, and make you more aware of what might be building up inside, so you can deal with it sooner and more directly. Softening your tone will lead you to talk in a calmer, more heartfelt way. Other people will be less able to shift the focus from *what* you're saying to *how* you're saying it. And you'll be in a stronger position to ask others to use a softer tone themselves.

How

Softening your tone doesn't mean becoming sugary or phony. Actually, when people shift away from being snippy, curt, derisive, or contentious, they usually become *stronger* communicators. They're now more grounded, more self-assured, when they bring up something. They haven't squandered interpersonal capital on the short-term gratifications of a harsh tone.

So try to be mindful of your tone, especially if you're already feeling stressed, pressured, frustrated, tired, or hungry. Consider the history of a particular relationship, and the sensitivity of the other person to your tone. Be on the lookout for negative tone, including in seemingly mild ways, such as an eye roll, an exasperated sigh, or a little put-down.

Consider your true purposes—in life, and with this other person. Does a harsh tone serve them? What kind of tone would serve them better? Can you say what is important without adding a negative tone to it? Can you deal with any hurt, anger, or practical issues in a straightforward way, rather than blowing off steam with your tone?

Give thought to your choice of words. Exaggerations, accusations, fault-finding, insults, swearing, alarming threats, patholo-gizing (for example, "You've got a personality disorder"), and cheap shots (for instance, "You're just like your father") are like pouring gasoline on hot coals. Try to avoid provocative or inflammatory language. Look for words that are accurate, constructive, self-respecting, and get to the heart of the matter.

Be careful with texts and emails. Once you push the "send" button, there is no getting it back, and the receiver may misinterpret it, and perhaps share it with others. Yes, it's old-fashioned, but it's certainly easier to repair any misunderstandings when we're talking with others face-to-face or over the phone. I look back on some of my own emails and wince years later.

People can be sarcastic, snarky, or teasing in playful ways. But sometimes humor disguises an underlying woundedness or anger, and other people can feel this. Or they might simply misinterpret what you said. You may have thought you were just joking, but that may not be how it lands on the other person.

Try to relax your eyes, throat, and heart. This will naturally soften your tone. I sometimes imagine that I'm being videotaped during an interaction and it might be viewed later at our kid's wedding—or my memorial service. Without getting paranoid about it, you might do the same; you don't have to be perfect, but if you were watching the videotape yourself, what would you like to see?

If you do slide into a harsh tone, clean it up as soon as possible—which could be a minute after you say it. Sometimes it works to explain—not justify or defend—the underlying reasons for your tone to put it in context; for example, "I apologize; I'm tired and hungry, and it's been a tough day." Take responsibility for your tone and its impacts, and recommit to a clearer, cleaner, more direct way of expressing yourself.

36

Don't Rain on the Parade

Let's say you've had a moment of inspiration, gotten a new idea, or felt some enthusiasm bubbling up inside. It could be something like a different slant on a project at work or what to do as a couple this Saturday. Your notions are not fully formed and you're not really committed to them yet, but you like them and are trying them on for size. Then, if others respond in a neutral or positive way, even if they raise some practical concerns, you'll likely feel supported and energized. But if their initial response is mainly negative, focusing on problems, constraints, and risks—*no matter how valid they are*—you might naturally feel at least a little deflated, put down, or obstructed. It's worth reflecting on how this may have happened to you as a child or an adult.

This works the other way, too. If people come to you with an idea, passion, or aspiration, and you start out with doubts and objections, they probably won't feel good, period—and not good about opening up to you in the future. Could this have happened in one of your relationships?

This can happen inside your own head as well. If you pour cold water over your hopes and dreams, you'll live cautiously between the lines, sure, but you'll never know what warmth and light might have spread if you'd let them catch fire. Do you back your *own* play, cheer on your own parade? Or are you too quick with doubts, limitations, cost analyses, and reasons why not?

How

The points here apply both to when you're reacting to the (even harebrained) ideas of others, and when you're responding to your own inspirations and enthusiasms. Additionally, you might ask someone to consider them if they start drizzling on your parade.

Notice any reflexive pulling back, naysaying, or buzzkilling when you or someone else gets happily excited about something. Be aware of any personal history with your parents or others who got into an elevated mood or a bit of grandiosity that led to trouble later—and how that history might be shaping your reactions to people and situations today that are actually quite different.

We hope that a friend, coworker, or partner will support a specific idea, plan, or dream of ours. But, more broadly, in a significant relationship, it's natural to want to feel that the other person is supportive *in general*: a "co-enthusiast" with you, who is inspired, passionate, and open to possibilities. Not someone who usually leads with what's wrong about an idea, but rather someone who starts with what's right about it. Not someone you have to drag along or keep pumping up like a balloon with a leak. Are there people who might wish that you were more of a co-enthusiast with *them*? Are there simple things you could do to bring more enthusiasm and support into those relationships?

Remember that you can always still say no. Just because there's some new proposal on the table doesn't mean you're locked into doing it. It's OK to be quiet while you let things air out and take more shape before you respond. Even if your deep-down view is that this new idea is insane, disastrous, or worse—you may not have to say anything at all and it will collapse on its own.

When you do communicate—to yourself or to another person—try to start with what's true or useful about their idea. It may be fine to stay with just these themes, and then see what the other person says. If you do have concerns, expressing them usually works best if they're both timely and wanted. (Ignore this suggestion if there's a compelling reason to do so, such as ensuring someone's safety.) Keep your concerns relevant to the matter at hand; for example, if the cost of an idea is a few hundred dollars, any problems with it do not include poverty in old age.

Look at your family and friends. Look at yourself. What parades—what longings of the heart, big dreams, promises deferred, crazy ideas that just might really work—are you eager to get started?

What could you do today and tomorrow to open pathways for them?

37

Give Them
What They Want

Relationships are built from interactions, and interactions are built from back-and-forths like volleys in tennis. A turning point in an interaction is when one person sends something they want across the net. (Our wants include wishes, needs, desires, hopes, and longings.) It might be simple and concrete, such as: *Please pass the salt.* Or it might be complex and intangible: *Please love me as a romantic partner.* Some people express their wants clearly, but many do not. The more important a want is, the more likely it will leak out slowly, or be expressed with distracting or confusing add-ons and emotional topspin.

Think of a significant relationship. How clearly have you expressed your wants in it? How do you feel when the other person makes a sincere effort to give you what you want?

When I reflect on these two questions myself, it makes me realize that it's not always easy to ask for what I want, especially if it makes me feel vulnerable—so I should cut others more slack for expressing their wants in vague, guarded, or euphemistic ways. Second, it makes me realize that I should generally try to give others what they want *if it's reasonable and possible.* Out of benevolence, doing this is kind and caring. Out of self-interest, it's also a good way to address their complaints, build goodwill, and put yourself in a stronger position to ask for what *you* want.

I do *not* mean giving people things that would harm them,

you, or others. And if they say what they want in rude, demanding, or threatening ways, then their want could be a nonstarter until they change their tone. For sure, you are free to decide what is reasonable in what the other person wants and how you are going to respond to it.

How

In almost any relationship, you are probably already giving the other person much of what they want. Tensions and issues arise around what *else* they want that they think they're not getting. Consider a significant relationship and ask yourself: *What else would they like from me?* Any wish or request that's gone unheard, any longing that hasn't been satisfied, means that they are not getting something they want. Anything that was disappointing for them, any ongoing source of friction: These also involve unfulfilled wants from their perspective.

It's scary and hard for many of us to express our most important wants. So try to sort through the surface clutter to the real priorities for the other person. What could be their softer, deeper, younger longings?

Once you have a sense of what the person wants, decide for yourself what, if anything, you are going to do about that. Your wants matter, too, and you can't keep giving without filling yourself up. If you've been raised in a family or culture that has said you should give, give, give to others, it's especially important to understand that this is not about you over-giving and running on empty. There's a sweet spot in which we're simply extending ourselves to the maximum *reasonable* extent for another person.

Most people want pretty straightforward things, such as:

I'd like more opportunities at work.

Please put the toilet seat down.

Ask me questions each day about myself, and pay attention to the answers.

Be nice to me.

Keep being my lover, even while we raise children.

Please return the shovel you borrowed.

Do your share of the housework.

Stick up for me with others.

Be interested in how I feel.

Tell me things you appreciate or like about me.

In many cases, it's really not that hard to give someone what they want. It's more a matter of whether *you* want to do it.

Personally, it was a great breakthrough to realize that giving others what they wanted was *not* knuckling under to them. Rather, it was a kind of triple-bonus aikido move that tapped into my caring for people while pulling me out of conflicts and putting me in the best position to ask for what I wanted myself.

You could pick something reasonable that you are not already doing, and just give it to the other person for an hour or a week without saying a word about it, and see what happens. Then pick something else to give and see what happens. In your mind or on paper, you could make a list of what has been at issue in that relationship and just work your way through it. If and when it feels right, talk about what you're doing with the other person. When you like, talk about your own wants (chapter 43, "Say What You Want"). Try this with one person after another.

This practice may seem like a high bar. But actually, when you make the shift, it's like walking downhill with the wind at your back. You are still taking care of your own needs and not letting people push you around. You're staying out of sticky quarrels by delivering the (reasonable) goods as best you can.

Consider what it's like to be with people who take care of themselves while giving you what you want as best they can. That's what it's like to be with *you* when you do the same yourself.

See Your Part

In situations or relationships with any kind of difficulty, it's natural to focus on what *others* have done that's problematic. This might be useful for a while, as it highlights what you care about. But there is also a cost: Fixating on the misdeeds of others is stressful. Plus it makes it harder to see their good qualities—and whatever might be your own part in the matter.

For example, let's say you work with someone who is unfairly critical of you. Meanwhile, they could be doing good things in other areas. Additional factors—such as coworkers who like to gossip—might be involved. And there might even be your own role as well, perhaps inadvertently.

To be clear, *sometimes we really do have no part in what happened*—like being hit by a drunk driver while you're walking across a street with a green light. In other situations, your own role might be small at most, and never justify the harmful actions of others. Knowing that you can recognize and, if need be, assert what is *not* your part gives you room to acknowledge what *is*.

We usually have more influence over ourselves than over other people. I've never been able to come to peace about anything that's bothered me until I take responsibility for whatever is my own part in it. Which, upon reflection, is sometimes nothing! But the *willingness* to see your own part can give you confidence in your sincere efforts and goodness, and knowing this about yourself is a real source of inner peace.

How

Since it may be challenging to look squarely at your own part in a situation, start by resourcing yourself: Bring to mind the feeling of being cared about; get a sense of some of your good qualities; and remind yourself of the benefits to you and others that will come from seeing your part.

Next, pick a challenging situation or relationship that involves another person . . . and take some time to consider:

- The ways that the person has truly mistreated you, and perhaps others.
- The ways that this person has perhaps benefited you and others.
- The effects of other people, society, and history.

Then consider your own role in the matter, whatever that might be. To do this, it helps to sort your actions—of thought, word, or deed—into the three groups we first explored in chapter 11 ("Forgive Yourself"):

- **Innocent**—Simply being there when something happened; not doing anything wrong; being accused of things you didn't do; getting targeted because of gender, age, ethnicity, appearance, or other sources of discrimination.
- **Opportunities for greater skillfulness**—Realizing that a certain word is understandably offensive to others; recognizing that you've overreacted to something; deciding to be a more engaged parent or to give your partner more attention.
- **Moral faults**—These are occasions when we violate our own deep code of integrity and deserve a wince of healthy remorse.

We all have moral faults, such as being unfair, demeaning others, nursing grudges, lying, treating people as if they didn't matter, abusing power, recklessness, or using coldness as a weapon.

The distinction between opportunities for greater skillfulness and moral faults is really important, and it applies both to yourself and to others you have issues with. Often, we miss chances to become more skillful because we think it will mean acknowledging a moral fault. Sometimes people accuse others of moral faults when it's really a matter of skillful correction—which usually makes the other person even less inclined to make that correction. To be sure, what is a matter of skillful correction for one person might appear to be a moral fault to another one; you have to decide for yourself.

As you take responsibility for your part, have compassion for yourself. Remember that surrounding that part are all sorts of good qualities in you—and seeing your part is another expression of your inherent goodness. Know these things, and let them sink in.

Allow waves of sadness or remorse to move through you as you see your part. Let them come, and let them go. Don't wallow in guilt: That actually undermines seeing and taking action about your own role. Remember that your part does not minimize the part of others. Appreciate that facing your part can sometimes help others to face their own.

Increasingly, try to find your way to a kind of peace. When you see your part with clarity and a whole heart, then you are not resisting anything. And no one can tell you something about your own role that you don't already know. There is relief, a softening and opening, an upwelling sense of your own good heart.

Then, gently, see if any actions come to mind that would be wise and helpful. Perhaps some communications to others, or resolutions about the future, or making amends. Take your time here; you can trust yourself to know what to do.

When you have a sense of the benefits of seeing your part, really take it in. You certainly deserve it! Acknowledging your own part in a difficult situation is one of the hardest—and I think most honorable—things a person can do.

39

Admit Fault and Move On

Recall a time someone mistreated you, let you down, spoke harshly, made a mistake, got a fact wrong, or affected you negatively even if that was not their intention. (This is what I mean, broadly, by *fault*.) If the person refused to admit fault, you probably felt dismayed, frustrated, and less willing to trust them in the future. Relationships are dragged down by unadmitted faults. On the other hand, if this person acknowledged their fault, that could have helped you feel safer, warmer toward them—and more willing to admit faults yourself.

One time I went out to dinner with our adult son and he called me on a certain—ah—intensity sometimes about my own opinions when he was growing up. I sputtered and deflected a while in response, but then had to admit the truth of what he was saying (and acknowledge him for his courage in saying it), and told him I wouldn't do that anymore. When I said this, he felt better and I felt better. And then we could move on to good things—like more sushi!

How

Remember that it's in your own best interests to admit fault and move on. Admitting fault might seem weak or that you're giving others a free pass for *their* faults. But actually, it takes a strong person to admit fault, and it puts you in a stronger position with others.

Inside your mind, sort out your fault from the other aspects of the relationship. Try not to make the fault bigger than it actually is. Be specific as to what the fault is. You are the final judge of this. Try not to get stuck in guilt or self-criticism; give yourself compassion and respect, as we've explored in part one.

Admit the fault clearly to the other person. Be simple and direct. You might describe the context—perhaps you were tired or upset about something else—but try to avoid justifying or excusing yourself. Sometimes, especially in charged situations, it's best to acknowledge your fault without any explanation wrapped around it.

Try to be empathic and compassionate about the consequences of your fault for the other person. You can remind yourself why this is good for *you* to do. Stay on the topic of the fault for a reasonable amount of time, but you don't have to let other people repetitively pound you for things you've already admitted.

If it's relevant, it might be useful to say how the other person could help you avoid this mistake in the future. For example, if they interrupted you less in meetings at work, it might be easier for you to keep an irritated tone out of your voice. If your co-parent did more of their share of housework and childcare, you might be more patient with sibling squabbles at the end of a long day. A useful structure for this is something like: *Truly, I don't want to do X again, and I take responsibility for that. I'm not blaming you for X. Also, just factually, it would help me if you did Y; that's my request.* Be careful at this point that you don't get into an angry counteraccusation about how they always do Y, and it's really bad, they're really bad, and so on. You're making a simple request—probably one that is obviously reasonable—and they will either do Y or they won't. You'll keep your eyes open and see what they do. Meanwhile, as best you can, avoid doing X.

Make a commitment to yourself, and perhaps to the other person, not to do this fault again. If you do slip, know that you will acknowledge it and recommit to avoiding the fault in the future. These commitments ensure that you're not making a mere gesture to get the other person off your back, and will give you self-respect while reassuring others.

When it feels right, disengage from discussing your fault. And then—sheesh!—it's time to move on. To more positive topics, and to more productive ways of relating with the other person. And move on to feeling lighter and clearer yourself.

40

Drop the Case

A few years ago, I was really caught up in a kind of "case" against someone. It was a combination of criticisms of them, irritations with others who hadn't stuck up for me, and feeling hurt underneath it all. It's not that I hadn't been mistreated—really, I had been. The problem was that my case was biased toward my own viewpoint, saturated with anger, and full of me-me-me. Every time I thought about it, I got worked up and upset. It felt awful. My case created issues with others who supported me but were leery of getting pulled into my rants. All my ruminating sucked attention and energy away from happier and more productive things.

In a difficult relationship, one or both people often have a detailed Bill of Particulars against the other person. It's painfully normal. Still, it's very useful to appreciate that you can see people clearly for who they are, recognize harms done to you or others, have compassion and support for yourself, and take appropriate actions . . . all without being hijacked by an angry, righteous case about someone.

How

Pick a challenging relationship, and see if you've got a case against that person. It's probably related to a grievance, resentment, or conflict. Step back from it and summarize it for yourself. Consider any ways that it's been intensified or shaped by your life history, including previous relationships stretching back to childhood. For example, as a quiet shy child, I was mad at the "cool kids" who led the groups that excluded me in school. Even today, those old feelings can stir up a strong reaction to being left out of something.

Next, consider these questions:

- What have been the "payoffs" to you in making this case? For example, perhaps your criticism of the other person has helped you avoid feeling really sad about what has happened in this relationship.
- What has it cost you—and perhaps others—to be caught up in this case? Perhaps it has disrupted your sleep, and put mutual friends in an awkward position.
- Are the benefits of making this case worth the costs?
- Can you bring some compassion to yourself now, as you reflect about all this?

Going forward, watch how various cases start forming in your mind, trying to get their hooks into you. You can feel the sense of them in your body, such as a pinched and irritated look in your face, a tightening in your belly, and a general sense of revving up. Then see if you can interrupt the process of case-making. Focus on the tender underlying feelings inside yourself and bring compassion to them. If your mind starts to go back to the verbal activity of the case, return your attention to your underlying feelings and body sensations.

Let the emotional charge of the case wash through you,

releasing, passing away. Let yourself see clearly, as if from a high mountaintop. Feel your own sincerity, your own good heart. Release the case, let go of it, like turning your hand over and dropping a heavy weight.

What a relief!

41

Stay Right When You're Wronged

It's easy to treat people well when they treat you well. The real test is when they treat you badly. It's natural to want to strike back. It might feel good—for a little while. But then the other person might overreact, too, and now you're in a vicious cycle. Other people could get involved and muddy the water. We don't look very good when we act out of upset, and others remember. It gets harder to work through issues in reasonable ways. When you calm down, you might feel bad inside.

So let's explore how you can stand up for yourself without the fiery excesses that have bad consequences for you and others.

How

You can use these suggestions both in the heat of the moment and as a general approach in a challenging relationship.

Get Centered

This step could take just a few breaths, or if you like, a few minutes. Here's a quick review of psychological first aid:

- **Pause**—You rarely get in trouble for what you *don't* say or do. When I work with couples, much of what I'm trying to do is to s-l-o-w them down to prevent runaway chain reactions.

- **Have compassion for yourself**—This is a sense of: *Ouch, that hurts. I feel warmth and caring for my own suffering.*
- **Get on your own side**—This is a stance of being *for* yourself, not against others. You're an ally to yourself, being strong on your own behalf.

Clarify the Meanings

What are the important values or principles that the other person may have violated? For example, on a 0–10 Awfulness Scale (a dirty look is a 1 and nuclear war is a 10), how bad was what the other person has done, or is doing? What meanings are you giving to events—and are they accurate and proportional to what has happened? Events do not have an inherent meaning; the meaning they have for us is the meaning *we* give them. If what has happened is a 3 on the Awfulness Scale, why have reactions that are a 5 (or 9!) on the 0–10 Upset Scale?

See the Big Picture

Take a moment to focus on your body as a whole . . . the room as a whole . . . lift your gaze to the horizon or above . . . imagine the land and sky stretching away from wherever you are . . . and notice how this sense of the wider whole is calming and clarifying. Then place what this person has done in the larger frame of your life these days. What they did could be a small part of that whole. Similarly, place what has happened in the whole long span of your life; here, too, it's probably just a small fraction of it.

Alongside the ways you've been wronged, what are some of the many, many things in your life that are good? Try to get a sense of dozens and dozens of genuinely good things, compared to whatever has been bad.

Get Support

When we've been mistreated, we need others to "bear witness," even if they can't change anything. Try to find people who can support you in a balanced way, neither playing up nor playing down what has happened. Get good advice—from a friend, a therapist, a lawyer, or even the police.

Have Perspective

In the next few chapters, I'll have specific suggestions for how to talk about difficult issues, resolve conflicts, and, if need be, shrink a relationship to a size that's safe for you. Here, I'm focusing on the big picture.

Listen to your intuition, to your heart. Are there any guiding principles for you about this relationship? Can you see any key steps to take that are under your own influence? What are your priorities, such as keeping yourself and others safe? If you wrote a short letter to yourself with good guidance in it, what might it say?

Recognize that some wrongs will never be righted. This doesn't mean minimizing or excusing bad behavior. It's just a reality that sometimes you can't do anything about it. When this is the case, see if you can feel the grief of damage that can never be repaired, with compassion for yourself.

Walk a Higher Road

When you've been wronged, it's especially important—even though it can be really difficult!—to commit to practicing unilateral virtue, as we explored in chapter 24 ("Take Care of Your Side of the Street"). Know what your own Dos and Don'ts are. With certain situations and people, it's helped to remind myself of specific "instructions," such as: *Stay focused—don't pursue their distracting accusations. Keep breathing. Stay measured and to the point. Don't feel that I need to "prove" or justify myself.* Also tune into the feeling of being calm and centered.

If you are going to be interacting with this person again, think through how you'd like to conduct yourself in specific situations, such as a family gathering, a performance review at work, or bumping into an ex- while you're with your current partner. You can mentally "rehearse" skillful responses to different things they might say or do. It might seem over-the-top, but practicing these in your mind will help you actually do them if things get intense.

Try to stay out of quarrels. It's one thing to work with someone toward the resolution of an issue. But it's a different matter to get caught up in recurring wrangles and squabbles. Quarreling eats away, like acid, at a relationship. I was in a serious relationship in my mid-twenties, but our regular quarrels finally so scorched the earth in my heart that the kind of love needed for marriage couldn't grow there.

If the other person starts getting fiery—speaking more loudly, getting provocative, threatening you, blasting you—deliberately step back from them, taking some long slow breaths, and keep finding that sense of calm strength inside yourself. The more out of control they get, the more self-controlled you can be.

Much of the time, you'll realize that *you just don't have to resist the other person.* Their words can pass on by like a gust of air swirling some leaves along the way. You don't have to be contentious. Your silence does not equal agreement. Nor does it mean that the other person has won the point—and, even if they have, would that actually matter so much in a week or a year?

If you find yourself driving, driving your point home, insisting that you're right and they're wrong, speeding up, coming in hot with guns blazing . . . try to have a little alarm bell go off inside that you've gone too far, take another breath, and regroup inside. You could then say what's on your mind in a less aggressive or all-knowing way. Say less to communicate more. Or you could stop talking, at least for a bit. I definitely have a tendency to hammer my point home, and then I try to remember the acronym I heard from a friend, WAIT: Why Am I Talking? (Or WAIST: Why Am I *Still* Talking?!)

You might acknowledge to the other person that you've gotten into a kind of argument, and then add that this is not what you really want to do. If that person tries to keep up the fight, you don't have to. It takes two to quarrel, and only one to stop it.

If you need to, stop interacting with the person who has wronged you—for a while, or permanently. Leave the room (or the building), get off the phone, stop texting. Know what your boundaries are, and what you'll do—concretely, practically—if someone crosses a line.

Be at Peace

Others are going to do whatever they do and, realistically, sometimes it may not be that great. Many people disappoint: They've got a million things swirling around in their head, life's been tough, there were issues in their childhood, their ethics are fuzzy, their thinking is clouded, their heart is cold, or they're truly self-centered and mean. It's the real world, and it will never be perfect.

Meanwhile, we need to find peace in our own hearts, even if it's not present out there in the world. A peace that comes from keeping eyes and heart open, doing what you can, and letting go along the way.

42

Talk about Talking

've worked with many people who have issues with each other. The specifics vary. But underneath it all, there was usually a single fundamental issue: They couldn't talk about their issues effectively. Voices would rise, the tone would get heated, someone would keep swerving away from the topic at hand, another person would blow up and derail the conversation, threats would be made, people would sit in sullen stony silence. In the extreme, there'd be yelling and screaming, children would look on in frightened horror, vicious things would be said, and sometimes someone would need to call the police.

Good process leads to good results; bad results come from bad process. If the results in our relationships are not so good, it's our *process* that needs improving.

When you talk about talking with other people, the focus moves away from the specific issues on the table, which could be charged, even explosive. You're stepping back to look at the relationship from a bird's-eye view, and this in itself can be calming. Then you can discuss how to speak to each other in ways that are more respectful and effective.

How

Shared Goals and Guidelines

Even if it's one particular person who keeps going off the rails, try to approach this as a "we" problem—and opportunity—rather than "me correcting you." Make it clear that the "rules of the road" will apply to both of you. Refer to your shared goals, such as cooperating in raising your kids even if you're divorced, having meetings at work that are productive, or having a harmonious friendship in which you each feel heard and respected. Emphasize your desire to understand the other person and to meet their needs as best you can, such as: *I do want to learn what I did here that landed so hard on you, and you could help me do that by not yelling at me.* Or: *Like you, I want to make sure that X does not fall through the cracks again, so can we pin down what led to that this time?*

Lower the Heat

If you need to talk about talking, things could already be charged and people might be defensive. So it's good to introduce this subject in ways that don't add to the tension. Focusing on the future will help, rather than criticizing the past. For example, you could say: *Going forward, when people make suggestions at work, could we start by saying what we like about their idea before getting into potential problems with it?*

Under certain conditions, you may need to be insistent, such as: *If you keep talking to me this way, I'm going to end this call.* But, in general, requests will be easier to hear than demands. For example: *I'm not trying to control how you speak. I'm just asking—it's a request, not an order—for the sake of our children, if we could talk with each other in a different way.*

Without blaming others, you could refer to your own needs or preferences, such as: *I had a very overbearing and loud stepfather, so when you become intense, that makes it hard for me to stay open to what you're saying.* Or you could frame your requests in terms of cultural differences—not good, not bad, just different—such as: *In your family, people are friendly and boisterous and talk over each other, which is all fine. I grew up with a different style, though, in which people were more uptight and took turns speaking. If we're just having fun, I like your style. On the other hand, if we're talking about something important—it's just my own background—but I'd appreciate it if you could hear me out before jumping in.*

By the way, my examples come from my own way of speaking, shaped by growing up in California and being a therapist, and you can adapt them to your own style and situation. While they might sometimes seem like walking on eggshells, I've learned (painfully) that being extra careful when you talk about talking can head off additional conflicts.

When to Put "Talking" on the Table

In the flow of a conversation or meeting, you could make little suggestions to get the process back on track. For example, you might ask, *Sorry, I've gotten a little lost. What's our topic here?* Or you might say, *I think we're getting a little heated—I know I am—so I hope we can slow down a bit.* Or you could be very direct with something like this: *Please, I won't interrupt you and I'd appreciate you not interrupting me.* Or: *If I bother you, could you talk with me about it instead of telling other people?*

If these on-the-fly comments are enough, great. If not, you could specifically focus on how you and the other person are interacting. If things are relatively friendly and informal, you might say something like this: *I've noticed that when we discuss X, we sort of bounce all over the place and don't really resolve it. I know I'm a big part of this. Can we talk about what might help us get to a conclusion?* On the other hand, if there are serious and explosive conflicts, it could be appropriate to say: *I'd like to meet with you and a therapist [or manager] to discuss how we speak to each other, and to set some ground rules for the future. When would be good for you?* Or you might say: *Because you are so angry and threatening, I'm no longer going to talk with you in person. I'm only going to communicate in writing, through texts and emails. If you send me anything abusive, I'm going to pass it along to my attorney.*

You do not need anyone's permission to talk about talking. Nor do you need their agreement to draw your own boundaries. You don't need to bend over backward to avoid the least possibility that the other person will say you are being critical of them. If they try to change the subject, you can come back to how you speak with each other.

Dos and Don'ts

Informally or formally, it can help to be concrete and specific about how you would like to speak with each other (applied to both of you). Here are some suggestions:

DO

- Practice "wise speech" (chapter 30, "Watch Your Words") by saying what is well-intended, true, beneficial, timely, not harsh, and (if possible) wanted.

- Start with empathy for each other's feelings.
- Say what you like or agree with before saying what you dislike or disagree with.
- Take some time to reconnect with each other when you get home from work before diving into problem solving.
- When appropriate, use a simplified form of the "nonviolent communication" developed by the psychologist Marshall Rosenberg: *When X happens* [stated specifically and objectively; not *When you are a jerk*], *I feel Y* [emotions; not *I feel you are an idiot*], *because I need Z* [deep needs such as: *to be safe, respected, emotionally close to others, not bossed around*].
- Take turns with each other's topics. Give each other roughly equal time to speak.
- Keep paying attention.
- Ask if this is a good time to talk.
- Think about your impact, even if unintended, on someone from a different background.
- Take a break if things are too heated; agree when to come back to the conversation to complete it, rather than avoiding it.

DON'T
- Gossip about each other or undermine each other with co-workers, friends, children, or family.
- Lie, bullshit, mislead, or deceive.
- Yell, scream, punch the wall, throw things.
- Swear or curse at each other.
- Call names, be insulting.
- Be condescending, patronizing, or disdainful.
- Jump full speed into a delicate topic.
- Argue when we're hungry, tired, or intoxicated.
- Throw in side issues, especially inflammatory ones.

- Stonewall, evade, or refuse to address certain topics.
- Get defensive or counterattack to avoid dealing with something.
- Ever, ever be violent or threatening.

You could write up your own version of Dos and Don'ts, and then post it on the refrigerator at home or send it to someone as your suggested ground rules for how you will talk with each other in the future. In a more extended way, you could find a book that you both like and agree to use it as a kind of manual for your relationship. There are many excellent guidebooks, and one of my favorites is *Say What You Mean* by the communications expert Oren Jay Sofer.

If you depart from the guidelines, acknowledge that and move back "inside the lines." If the other person departs from them, it's usually important to call that out, and ask the person to return to them. Otherwise, they'll think that it's fine to go outside the lines. If someone says that they want to improve their process with you but they keep breaking the rules, that fact rises to the top of the list of what is important to address with them. If they still keep violating your boundaries, then you could need to disengage from them as much as possible.

You can let little stuff slide by, and be OK with a natural, loose style of talking as long as it doesn't get abusive. But, overall, be serious about how others speak to you and how you speak to them, and serious about how interactions unfold, especially in significant relationships. You have legitimate rights and needs. Almost certainly, many other people would want to be treated in the ways that you are asking for. You're not being overly sensitive or a "snowflake." You're seeking the greater good in your interactions and relationships, and are willing to abide by the rules yourself.

43

Say What You Want

We're born wanting. From the first breath, we want comfort, food, and the sense of others who are caring. Children want things from their parents. And we want things from them—such as going back to sleep at 3 a.m.! Wanting is natural. Because we depend on each other, of course we want things from each other.

As we move through childhood and into adulthood, our wants become more complex. Expressing them can become emotionally charged, guarded, or suppressed. Common as this is, it's a central bottleneck and roadblock in relationships. You can't make agreements with others about what you want if you can't say what that is.

How

We'll be focusing here on how you can clarify and communicate *your* wants. This could also help you better understand and respond to the wants of others. After you go through this chapter as it applies to yourself, you could think about a significant person in your life and consider what they might want in general—and, in particular, from you.

Be Mindful of Wanting

Some wants are easy to express, such as: *Please open the door.* Wants where more is at stake are potentially riskier to talk about, and thus harder to say. Depending on the situation, examples include:

I'd like more of a leadership role on this team.

I want more credit for my accomplishments in this company.

I wish you'd give me your full attention when we talk.

Can you be affectionate without it always getting sexual?

I need more alone time.

You need to do your share of the dishes.

Can we make love once or twice a week?

I don't want to have kids and I know you do.

We need to save more money for when we're both retired.

I feel sad and would just like some comforting.

I want to give you all the love in my heart.

As you read the examples above, were there any that made you kind of wince or pull back, perhaps with a thought like, *Whoa, I couldn't say that.* It's normal to have feelings and inhibitions that bottle up what we want and how we talk about it. For example, well into my twenties it was very hard to express my longings to be loved.

Try to be mindful of the feelings and perhaps blocks that come up for you when you get close to saying something important that you want. For instance:

- There might be a tension in your throat, a hollow feeling in the pit of your stomach, a mounting anxiety, a dread of the other person's reactions, or a sense of defeat in advance in a relationship with recurring conflicts.
- Notice any swerving away from being forthright and direct, such as using euphemisms, vague or abstract terms, or superficial proxies for what you really care about (for example, fixating on the single wrong word someone used, rather than making a vulnerable request for more respect in general).
- Be aware of any connections to how you were raised; for example, an avoidance of topics such as sex or money. How did your mom and dad express their wants? How did they respond when you expressed your own?
- Consider how you've been socialized in terms of gender, social class, race, religion, or the general culture in which you grew up or now live. What are people "like you" supposed to want, and how are they supposed to talk about it?

As you deepen awareness of your reactions to wanting, they will have less power over you, and you'll be better able to say what you really want.

Know What You Want

Imagine a very kind and supportive person—it might be someone you know, a teacher, or a spiritual being—asking you what you truly want from life in general, and also regarding certain relationships, situations, or issues. What do you want from particular people? How do you wish they would feel about you? What do you wish they would say or do? Think about past events that went badly, such as a big argument; what do you wish the other person had done differently—and would do differently in the future? Take some time with these questions. In your mind or on paper, what answers come up for you? In this exercise, what does it feel like to express your wants fully, in a safe and receptive space, and to have them deeply heard by this imagined being? You can trust and value this feeling, and look for people with whom you can have at least some sense of it, and do what you can to nudge your interactions with them to give you an even greater sense of this.

What we want usually has two aspects to it: (1) an *experience* that is (2) the result of an *action* or *situation*. The experience itself is the gold, and the action or situation is a means to that end. For example, you might want someone to value your opinion more at work: that valuing—shown through praise or just a tone of respect—is a means to the end of the experience of feeling worthy, included, or wanted. This seemingly obvious point has huge implications: It means that *we are not so bound to particular actions or situations in order to have the experiences we long for.* There could be many ways for you to feel worthy, valued, and cared about. We can get fixated on particular people saying particular things in particular ways in order to have a desired experience. If they do this, fine, but if not, where does that leave you? So when you explore your wants, keep highlighting the *experiences* that you seek, including their deeper, softer layers. Try to identify a variety of things that others could do that would foster these experiences. Then there's more flexibility in what you'll be asking of them—and more likelihood that you'll have the experiences you want.

It's helpful to be as clear and concrete as you can about what you'd like others to *do*. This clarity has multiple benefits, including:

- Reducing potential misunderstandings.
- Giving you a sense of self-respect that you've really said it.
- Often reassuring others that what you're asking for is doable.
- In conflict situations, putting others on notice; you will then know that they know, with unmistakable clarity, what you want.
- Providing a solid basis for making agreements, and an easy way to tell if the agreement has been kept.

Think about an important relationship, perhaps one with significant challenges. What would it look like if they gave you what you wanted? For example, at work, what would they say about you in a meeting? What salary would they pay you? How would they support you in the company? At home, how many nights a week would they make dinner? What tone would they never use with your children? How would they touch you? When would you make love?

Try to turn vague feelings into specific requests. Suppose you'd like to feel "better" around someone. What does that mean? What could they do that would help you feel better around them? Perhaps a warmer tone of voice, less criticism, and more acknowledgment of your contributions. In most relationships, even at work, you could ask for these things. Suppose you wish your partner and co-parent would "help more" at home? What does that actually mean? Perhaps the "more" would be sweeping the kitchen each night, and taking the lead in figuring out what to do about your third-grader's issues with reading.

What we want from others includes what happens inside their minds, not just what they say and do. Depending on the situation, you might wish that someone were more patient, more committed to their sobriety, more interested in your inner world, or more willing to take responsibility for their part in a conflict. This doesn't mean becoming the Thought Police. Much as you can call yourself to a higher road inside your own mind, you can ask others to do the same.

Tell Them

We often express wants implicitly, such as leaning into a partner for a hug. If a look or a hint is enough, super. But if it's not, then you need to be more explicit. In the next chapter, we'll explore how to come to agreement about what you and others want. Here we are focusing on how to put your wants on the table.

The harder it is to talk about something, the more important it is to support yourself before you get started. You could draw on the chapters in part one, such as finding a sense of calm strength, accepting yourself, and knowing that you're a good person. Imagine that a wise being is sitting with you as you start to speak, respecting and encouraging you. If you can, find a sense of goodwill for the other person; you're not out to get them, even if what you want might make them uncomfortable.

As best you can, establish a foundation with the other person. In their groundbreaking work with couples, John and Julie Gottman found that a slower, softer transition into an important topic usually went better than abruptly and intensely jumping in. As appropriate, take some time to establish an emotional connection. Talk about neutral or pleasant topics first. Is there some appreciation or warmth toward them you could express? How is it going for the other person these days? You want them to listen to you, so it's wise to listen to them. This is not being manipulative, which involves deception; what you are saying is genuine for you, even if alongside it is the purpose of laying a foundation for a deeper conversation.

The brilliant couples therapist Terry Real emphasizes a framework of "us," rather than "you" over there and "me" over here. You could introduce the topic of what you want in this context, describing it as it relates to supporting your relationship with each other and your common goals. In a work setting, this might sound like: *I value our working relationship and have a suggestion as to how we could be more effective together. Could we talk about that? And, if not now, when would be a better time for you?* With a partner, you might say: *You're really important to me and how we are together also affects our kids. I've felt a little unsettled recently, and I'd like to talk about how we could make things better. OK?*

Reestablishing the frame of "us" over the course of a conversation can help, especially if it's starting to feel like either or both of you are retreating to your separate corners with shields up. Try to get the consent of the other person to have this conversation, rather than just sweeping them into it. They might feel that there is a criticism built in to what you want, and the frame of "us," along with getting their consent, could help them be more comfortable and open. Still, you have the right to say what you want even if they really, *really* don't want to hear it.

As you move into your topic, it might help to mention the

experiences you are seeking, emphasizing what is normal and universal. For example, at work you might say something like this to your manager: *I'd be happy to be given even more challenging projects in the future; I like the feeling of stretching myself and that I'm making a difference for our team.* With a romantic partner, you might say: *I know you care about me, and still, I'd like to hear you say it a little more, which would make me feel really good inside.* If it feels right, you could push yourself to be brave enough to reveal the deepest longings in your heart, such as: *You are special to me, and I want to feel that I am special to you.*

Talk about the past if you need to, but, as much as you can, *turn complaints about the past into requests for the future.* People can argue forever about what actually happened, who did what, and how big a deal it was. But you don't have to fight about the past to agree about what you'll do *from now on.* It's incredibly hopeful! And when you put your wants in terms of requests, they are easier for others to hear without feeling bossed around. You usually cannot force people to do anything. But you *can* ask them clearly, persuasively, and, if need be, firmly. You are not being a pushover when you make a request. You will watch and see what they do, and then decide how you are going to respond.

If the other person keeps bringing up the past or blaming you, you can refocus on the future, as in this sample dialogue:

PERSON A: I really don't like it when we yell at each other, and I'd like it to stop.

PERSON B: You're the one who's always yelling at me!

A: [thinks: *That is* so *not true; argh; but arguing about the past will distract from what I want going forward.*]

Whatever has happened in the past, I want us to stop yelling at each other from now on. Personally, it's really upsetting to me.

B: You're blaming me again for upsetting you.

A: I don't like it when *I* yell, not just when you yell. I'm not going to yell at you anymore and I'm asking you not to yell at me. OK?

B: I never yell. You're exaggerating.

A: Then it won't be a problem for us not to yell at each other. Right, no yelling from now on?

B: Yeah sure, whatever.

A: This is really important to me. You say that you do not yell at me. I appreciate that, and I am not going to yell at you.

B: You're always trying to control me. Just like you're so controlling with our son.

A: [thinks: *Wow, that's a low blow, and bringing in our son to boot. Things are happening here that I may want to talk about later on, but right now I'm going to stay focused on not yelling.*] I'm definitely trying to *affect* our relationship so there is no yelling in it. If that's controlling, it's applied to both of us. I'm just glad that we are not going to be yelling at each other from now on. Really, I appreciate you being willing to talk with me about this. I think it's going to be good for our relationship and our family.

In the dialogue above, Person A did not chase any side issues, and was unapologetic about wanting something—in this case, an end to yelling. It can be scary to say what we want, and potentially threatening and irritating for another person to hear it. Any want that's important enough to talk about probably has an emotional charge on it for both of you. Keeping that charge in mind, and helping yourself to stay centered and calm as you say what you want, will make it more likely that you actually get it.

44

Come to Agreement

Many situations highlight the need for agreements, such as changing roles inside a team at work, having children, or getting a new roommate. Most of our arrangements with others are not already established. We must *construct* them through a process of agreement.

When we make good agreements and revise them as needed, relationships go well and we can build wonderful things together. But when we can't come to agreement, conflicts fester and opportunities are lost. Relationships are founded on trust, and the basis of trust is mutual agreement. When agreements are broken and not repaired, or they are repeatedly misunderstood, or when one person won't make the most fundamental agreement of all—to *keep* one's agreements—that shakes the foundation of any relationship, sometimes to the point of ending it.

As someone who's prickly about being controlled, it helped me to realize that agreements can actually be freeing. They prevent issues from hijacking time and attention in a relationship, commit others to the support you need, and give you a platform of trust that you can launch from in life.

How

Find Common Ground

Suppose you're in a typical situation at work or at home in which you're trying to agree about something. The topic might be how much TV is OK for your kids to watch, what your manager is going to do to help you get a promotion, or whether you and your partner should try to move to a safer neighborhood. Maybe somebody is pushing you to do something that you're not sure about—or you're the one doing the pushing. Perhaps you're asking for a certain kind of emotional support. Think about things that you'd like from others but aren't getting, since they haven't yet agreed to them. Let's say you've said what you want, or they have. Now what?

A good first step is to emphasize where you already agree. What are the facts you both see, the things you both care about, the values you hold in common? As you manage differences, look for similarities. For example, you both could be on the same page about having an effective work group, being civil in meetings, or raising healthy and happy children. People are often aligned on the *ends* even if they differ about the *means*. So try to highlight the goals you share, both at the beginning of a discussion and if arguments about methods get heated.

If another person puts an idea on the table, you could begin by saying what you like about it. Try to narrow the range of a disagreement so it is more manageable. For example, at work you might say something like this: *I like your new PR strategy, though I'm concerned about its price tag.* With a divorced co-parent, it might be: *We're going to be dating new people—weird, right?—but I don't think we should introduce them to the kids unless it's a seri-*

ous relationship. With a friend, you might say: *Definitely, let's have lunch. I just need to be able to eat outside.*

I tend to be pretty detached, analytic, and fix-it oriented. (You've probably noticed!) So I try to remember a kind of mantra: *Start by joining*—with empathy, shared views and values, noting where you already agree, and carving out and bounding any issue that remains.

Negotiate Effectively

In even the strongest and happiest relationships, there is always some negotiating. Here are some things that help negotiations go well. To make them concrete and relevant, consider a recurring conflict with someone and how the suggestions below could apply to it.

Tackle One Issue at a Time

As tempting as it may be to move from one grievance to another, blend them together, or throw a whole kitchen sink full of complaints at someone . . . that's not very effective. Instead, pick one issue, name it, stay focused on it, and try to resolve it. In a natural flow, you may need to deal with its deeper layers, but it's still the same issue. You might say to a friend: *I felt hurt by your comment on my Facebook post, but this is not about particular words. It's about being friends who are kind to each other.* If another matter emerges that has to be resolved first, make the transition clear to it and flag that you will still have to return to the original concern. For example: *Oh boy, you're right, we have to decide how to handle the brake job our car needs, but once we figure that out, let's get back to where we'll be driving to on our vacation.*

A kind of meta-issue in relationships is who gets to put their issues on the table, and whose issues get prioritized for attention and resolution. Do what you can to highlight your own topics, and push back against any internal—or external—pressures against doing this. *You have a voice and it deserves to be heard.* If you want to talk about X but the other person wants to talk about Y, decide who goes first—with the clear understanding that you will get to each of your topics. If need be, say in advance how much time you'll spend on each issue. It might be helpful to start with their issue, to clear the decks and build initial goodwill, if possible.

If somebody keeps bringing up side issues, you could point that out—and return to your topic. If other people say things that are not relevant to your topic—such as a snarky comment about one of your friends, or a suggestion about an unrelated matter—generally let them go by, though maybe with a mental note to come back to them later on. Keep returning to where there is the potential of making a new good agreement. Stay focused on the result you are aiming for. For instance, we don't have to zing people about the past while they're agreeing with us about the future.

If you start to get the feeling that the other person doesn't intend to make any agreement with you, period, then try to talk about that. You might say: *Maybe I'm wrong, but do you actually want to find some kind of agreement here with me? Are you mad at me and is this a bad time to try to solve one of our issues? Or do you just not want to be pinned down to anything at all?* Hopefully, talking about this will get you both back into the frame of coming to agreement. And, if not, you could take a break and come back to this later. Or, if need be, and perhaps sadly, you might have to re-evaluate this relationship and lower your expectations for what you can count on from the other person.

Pin It Down

People can argue forever about lofty values or abstract ideas, such as what *equity* means in a workplace, how *permissive* parents should be with their kids, or what is *being nice*. Instead, try to be concrete and specific, especially if there is a history of misunderstanding—or, frankly, evasiveness and slipperiness. For example, how long will a meeting be at work, what's the agenda, and what are the roles of the people attending it? At home, what are the expectations about housework, children, pets, and whether to put the cap back on the toothpaste? In a couple that's sharing finances, what might seem initially like a big divide between a "tightwad" and a "big spender" could boil down to a difference of $20 a week in what they want to spend on eating out—much more manageable.

Bounding and concretizing what you are asking for could help the other person realize that it may not be such a big deal to do that for you. It's often remarkably easy to resolve an issue and make other people happy. For example, if your partner wants more heart-to-heart conversations, spending twenty minutes a few times a week to do that could be plenty. You can make it clear that you will be truly satisfied if the other person just does X or Y or Z.

Be clear about what each person is going to do, and when, and how. You could say what you think you are agreeing to, and you could ask them to do the same. Try to minimize any fuzziness or ambiguity, which make it all too easy for someone eventually to feel let down.

Give to Get

Most of our relationships involve exchanges of one kind or another. This doesn't mean keeping score second by second, but over the long haul there's a reasonable balance of give-and-take. So try to find out what you could do that would incline the other person in your direction. With a friend, you might say: *If I do the driving, can we go to my favorite restaurant?* At work, you might say: *Thanks for doing this report, and I'm happy to make copies of it for the meeting.* In general, you could ask this simple, powerful question: *What would help you give me what I'm asking for?*

Big issues are often linked together, and it's OK to make a kind of deal about them. For example, a classic pattern in romantic relationships is *pursuer/distancer*: the more that one person tries to get close, the more the other person steps back . . . which naturally makes the first person want to hold tighter than ever. So the pursuer might say, *I'm going to give you more space,* and the distancer could reply, *Thanks, and I'm going to be better about saying that I love you.* When a couple have children, sometimes one parent would like better teamwork while the other one hopes to restore their intimate relationship, and it might help to address both these needs together. I remember a parent joking to me: *Foreplay starts when my partner makes the kids' lunches in the morning.*

In a significant relationship, even if what you want is a matter of mere preference or even if the other person doesn't understand why you would ever want *that* . . . they could still choose to give you what you want because, um, they care about you. Taking this approach can be an effective way to get out of arguing about the specific merits of something you want, and instead go to a higher level that is about your general caring for each other.

Consolidate Gains

As you resolve one issue, it may be tempting to zoom onto another one. But that might rattle the hornet's nest just when things were starting to settle down. It could be stressful and tiring to talk through issues, so it might be wise to acknowledge the progress you've achieved, and not exhaust the other person and make them reluctant to talk with you about agreements in the future.

Large issues are often resolved through a series of small agreements. In your mind, you could map out a progression of steps that build on each other, gathering momentum, and strengthening trust along the way.

Address Broken Agreements

When an agreement is broken, it's important to name that this has happened. Otherwise, the broken agreement will become the new standard—and keeping agreements in general will seem like less of a priority in your relationship. If you broke the agreement, acknowledge this openly, and either recommit to the agreement or suggest a revised version that would be easier for you to keep.

If the other person broke the agreement, find out why. You can start carefully, not jumping in with a fiery accusation. Was there a genuine misunderstanding about what exactly had been agreed to? For example, one person might think that the "end of the week" for turning in a report meant Friday while for the other person it was Sunday night. Were there some factors that got in the way of keeping the agreement—for instance, it just takes longer to complete an errand during rush-hour traffic—and which you should take into account in the future? Was someone simply forgetful? Or was the other person never really committed to the agreement in the first place? Or, even worse, do they just not care about keeping their promises to you? These are questions you need answers to.

If an agreement was broken due to a misunderstanding, an unforeseen circumstance, or simple forgetfulness, it's usually straightforward to reestablish it, perhaps with some modifications. But if it becomes clear that the other person doesn't take their agreements seriously—perhaps shown by downplaying their broken promise to you, getting defensive, making it somehow your fault, or counterattacking because you've dared to talk about what they've done—*then that rises to the top as the key issue.* You can stay (relatively!) calm and centered as you deal with this, drawing on what we've previously explored in this book. Sometimes other people do some harrumphing and grumbling while grudgingly recommitting to an agreement . . . and then actually keep it going forward. You may need to be quite direct, even grave to get through to a person who has a cavalier attitude about agreements. If this is the case, at work you might say, *No, I'm not like your last manager; when you tell me you'll get something done by a certain date, I expect that to happen.* With a partner you might say, *Could you treat your agreements with me and your children as seriously as you do those at work?* Depending on the situation, you might need to get very blunt: *I'm committed to keeping my agreements with you. I can't make you keep your agreements with me. But I can tell you that if you don't, I'm going to disengage from this relationship because, frankly, I won't be able to trust you.*

Agreements matter. Respecting the ones you make and asking the people in your life to do the same is a way of treating yourself like *you* matter, and others as well.

45

Resize the Relationship

Relationships have foundations, such as shared understandings and values. If a relationship is smaller than its foundations, that's an opportunity to enlarge it if you'd like. On the other hand, if a relationship is bigger than its true foundations, that creates risks for you and perhaps others.

Resizing relationships is a natural process. With a casual acquaintance, you might learn that you've both had health issues, giving you an opportunity for a deeper connection. Or perhaps a longtime friend tells you to just get over it a month after your beloved dog dies, so you take a step back from them. Sometimes there is a basic difference between one person and another. Neither of you is right or wrong; it's simply that (let's say) the other person is never going to be as extroverted as you, or as interested in art and music—so you start spending less time together.

Imagine a circle that represents all the possibilities with another person when you first meet. And then things happen that lead you to carve out certain parts of that circle, reducing the scope of the relationship and how it can affect you. For example:

> *Hmm, our politics are at opposite ends of the spectrum, easier not to talk about it.*

> *After that first date, I'm not interested in romance here.*

They're fun, but I don't like to go to bars with them.

Not much emotional support when I really need it; not going to ask for it again.

I'm not ready to leave this relationship, but I sure don't want to get married.

I'm going to stick this out until the kids go off to college, and then take a really hard look at our relationship.

I love my dad and am going to take care of him, but he just can't live with us.

Resizing can actually support a relationship. You don't have to cut off all contact—though, if you choose, it may come to that—to have a relationship that you like for what it is, whose size and shape are based on what you can truly trust and expect from the other person. You have the right to resize things as you judge best. Knowing that you have this right could make you more comfortable with expanding a relationship, since you know that you can shrink it if needed. It's also easier to sustain some relationships—rather than end them—when they're more circumscribed.

How

Take Stock

To create a context, ask yourself: *In general, how do you want other people to treat you, realistically? What do you feel you deserve in your relationships? What's your vision of healthy, sane, and happy relationships at work and at home, with friends and neighbors?*

Then think about a relationship that's challenging for you, and how it might be helpful to resize it. Depending on the situation, this resizing could look like shorter dinners with relatives, having another person in the room when you meet with someone at work, not talking about religion with a friend, saying a pleasant hello (but no more) as you pass in the hallway, letting a casual friendship gradually fade, ending a romantic relationship, never again exposing a vulnerability to a particular person, not returning someone's calls any more, or letting go of any hope for healing between you and a relative.

For this relationship, take your time and consider: Are certain topics particularly charged and a source of friction? Do they keep asking for certain things from you that you just don't want to offer? Do you want things from them that they're half-hearted at best about doing? Are certain situations a setup for trouble? In what ways might you have been asking more of them than they're capable of delivering? What are the recurring sources of tension, frustration, and disappointment? When the chips are down, will they do the right thing if it's hard?

On the other hand, when does the relationship go well? What is it safe to talk about? What can you trust about them? In what ways do they care about you? How are they loyal to you? Does this person have a learning curve in the social and emotional parts of their life? When you observe the relationship from a big-picture, bird's-eye view, are there things that you could do on your own—drawing on the previous chapters in this book—that could resolve any of the issues you've noted above, without having to shrink the relationship?

Consider how much this relationship actually matters to you. Do you need to stay on good terms with the other person because of your job or a family relationship (for instance, a father-in-law)? At the other end of the range, would it be OK with you if you never saw them again? How much effort do you want to put into repairing or managing an ongoing issue . . . or would you rather just disengage from that part of the relationship? Would you like to end it entirely?

It may feel quite sober, haunting, and sad to review a relationship in this far-reaching way. Be careful that you're not jumping to conclusions or letting a recent interaction cloud your view. Still, you can see what you see. The best predictor of the future is the past, and long-standing patterns are typically slow to change, if at all. You can feel gratitude, respect, love, and compassion alongside a cool clarity about another person and the sort of interactions and relationship you can realistically have with them.

Repair What You Can

After you take stock in these ways, essentially you have three choices: accept what the other person says and does and let it be, try to repair things, or shrink the relationship. If you decide on a repair, you could draw on the many tools we've explored. For example, if you feel routinely let down by someone in a certain area—perhaps they never call on you in a meeting—you could say what you want and try to come to agreement, as we discussed in the previous two chapters.

If there has been a major breach of trust—such as lying, infidelity, covert drug use, or misusing money you hold in common—I think that any meaningful repair must include responsibility and remorse from the other person, who must give you what you need to know that *this will never happen again.* If people start waffling on what they actually did to you, downplaying it, or saying you need to move on, it's hard to know if you can trust them again, which probably means that you're better off shrinking the relationship.

If there is a basic difference between you about something—such as how clean and tidy you want to keep the home you share, how much you like having deep emotional conversations, or your natural desires for sex—you can see if you could each stretch for the other and find some middle ground. While we have our natural "set points," human beings are psychologically flexible and capable of generating an interest in many different things. Knowing this, the particular issue itself—perhaps tidiness, conversation, or sex—becomes secondary, and the primary question is this: *Do you care enough about me and our relationship to nudge your mind in this way?* This is the central matter—and the other person might ask you a similar question. For example, in an inquiring—not accusatory—way, you could say things like this: *Is our relationship a priority for you? Could you ask me more about myself when we talk, and be interested in my answers? Once a week or so, could you deliberately stir up erotic feelings for me and be moved to initiate some intimacy? Because I matter to you, would you be willing to stay mentally engaged with the huge hassles in getting my mom settled in an assisted-living facility?*

When you make these efforts, you'll observe how it goes and what other people actually do. You'll see what kind of issues (if any) they can handle talking about. You'll see their real capacity for repair, including taking responsibility for their part, having empathy for you, staying civil, and talking through an issue. Relationships naturally need repairs. If the other person ignores or punishes your efforts at repair, that's a yellow flag in any significant relationship. If you can, try to talk about repair itself, and why it's important. For example, you might say: *Because I value our friendship, I'm trying to resolve something that's been awkward between us. That's why I'm bringing it up. I hope we can talk about it effectively. Could we do that? How do you think we should talk about this?* Hopefully, you will be able to mend things. But if the other person refuses to repair the lack of repair *in general*, that's a definite red flag in a relationship, and usually a clear sign that you need to resize it.

Grieve the Loss

There might be the loss of a love you hoped for, or a life together after the children have left home. Perhaps you realize that a business or project will not succeed because other people don't have the talent or drive needed to make it work. Maybe a friend is just never going to understand why you care so much about what you eat. You might have a boss who will not promote you.

Facing limitations in a relationship can make us feel angry, anxious, and deeply sad. Because this reckoning is often painful, people may try to defer it with wishful thinking or sheer avoidance. Occasionally, things get better on their own. But, as the saying goes, *Hope is not a plan.* It helps to have a kind of healthy disenchantment in which you wake up and see things clearly, even if that's painful.

Along the way, let yourself feel what you feel, with compassion and support for yourself. The classic stages of facing death, outlined by psychiatrist Elisabeth Kübler-Ross, offer a loose (and simplified) road map for this process: denial, bargaining, anger, despair, and then—hopefully—acceptance. Acknowledge your loss. And then, when it feels right, turn toward what is *also* true.

Turn toward the things that are good in this particular relationship, even as you disengage from what's been bad for you. Turn toward the good in other relationships and the world at large. You're not avoiding the pain of the loss. Actually, by turning toward what is good you'll be strengthening yourself to bear the things that are painful and sad.

There is a particular kind of loss when other people resize *their* relationship with you in ways that you don't like. If you can talk about it with them and perhaps make a repair, that's good. On the other hand, cold and sometimes emotionally brutal cutoffs are shockingly common. Perhaps you were dating someone who, without warning, starts ghosting you; your father says he wants nothing to do with you; your adult daughter stops returning your calls or refuses to let you see your grandchildren; your sibling makes up stories about you and won't say why; or certain relatives now refuse to break bread with you at the same table because you disagree about politics. In these sorts of unilateral estrangements—some of which I've personally experienced—it can help to:

- Find out what you can about why this has happened.
- Identify your own part in the matter, whatever it is—which might be nothing.
- Try to talk about it with the other person, if they're willing to.
- Learn what you can about what's going on with them, independent of you.
- Try to accept the loss, keep letting go, and disengage emotionally from the relationship.
- Turn toward what is still good; for example, you might come to feel that your true parents in this life are not the ones who conceived you.

Still, as wise about all this as you may be, getting exiled by someone you cared about is inherently wrenching. It may take years to come to a kind of peace about it. Sometimes all you can do is live as well as you can in the other parts of your life, and bear the pain that comes when you think of this other person.

Draw Your Boundaries

A key form of resizing happens when we more or less give up about a certain aspect of a relationship while still appreciating the person as a whole. With almost everyone, certain things will be missing for you. (This will be true for others about you, and it's humbling and honest to face it, and perhaps talk about it.) Depending on the kind of relationship you have, perhaps you will not be able to share a spiritual practice, it won't work to do a business project together, or the sex will be good but not great. Perhaps your efforts to get something to happen have been stressing the relationship and creating conflicts in it.

Or you might be in a situation in which you have to maintain contact with someone but inside your mind you take a big step back. You could be appropriately civil and pleasant while refusing to argue about certain topics, work on any future projects together, or be stuck in the same car together. Some people try to connect through bickering or by triggering an emotional reaction in others; if so, you can veer away from playing those roles in their scripts. Think about the bait they toss your way and how you've gotten pulled in previously, and what you could do from now on to steer clear of those interactions. Maybe you need to show up for certain occasions, such as a holiday dinner, while reserving the right to leave if people get too tipsy.

Many of the boundaries we set are implicit, without announcing or explaining them to the other person. That's often fine and appropriate, in part because it can avoid conflicts about why you are setting the boundary. On the other hand, you might want to declare yourself. If you do, you may choose to give the reasons you are taking this step, though it might be simplest to state the boundary and leave it at that, and stay out of arguments about it. Depending on the relationship, you might say:

I need to leave work by 5:30 p.m. to get home in time for dinner with my kids.

I can't lend you any more money.

I'm going to stay friends with _____, although you don't like them.

If you use that kind of language again, I'm leaving.

If you act like you might hit me, I'm calling 911.

I'm not going to do more than half the housework in this family.

If we're going to get intimate, I need a foundation of feeling loved by you that's not about sex.

No, I'm not going to have Thanksgiving with the uncle who molested me.

I want you to see your grandchildren, but please follow our rules about what you feed them.

If I find drugs in your bedroom, I'm flushing them down the toilet.

I don't want to talk about God any more.

I don't like watching football, and that's OK.

If you want to tell someone about a boundary, it may help to get the words clear in your mind (and perhaps on paper) before you say it. Fundamentally, you have the right to set boundaries and resize a relationship. Claiming this right—and, frankly, this power—is especially important if you haven't had your boundaries respected in the past. Nedra Tawwab's book *Set Boundaries, Find Peace* is an excellent guide to boundary-setting, both the inner attitudes and the outer skills, and draws from Tawwab's deep background as a therapist and relationships expert.

In the resizing process, it may be tempting to be vindictive and punishing. In the short run, this might feel good, but in the long run you'll regret it. I have. Even if you need to disengage entirely from another person, try to act in such a way that you'll be able to pass them on the street without feeling upset about it.

46

Forgive Them

Forgiveness has two distinct meanings:

- To give up resentment or anger
- To pardon an offense; to stop seeking punishment

I'm going to focus on the first of these, which includes situations in which you may not be ready to give someone a full pardon, but you'd still like to come to peace about what has happened. Finding forgiveness can go hand in hand with pursuing justice. It's possible both to view an action as morally reprehensible and to let go of anger at the person who did it. You might continue to feel sad at the impacts on you and others—and to take action to make sure it never happens again—while no longer feeling aggrieved, reproachful, or vengeful.

Forgiveness may seem lofty, like it only applies to big things, such as crimes or adultery. But most forgiving is for the small bruises of daily life, the times when others let you down, thwart or hassle you, or just rub you the wrong way.

The person who gains the most from forgiveness is often the one who does the forgiving. Sometimes we forgive people who never know we've forgiven them; they may not have known we felt wronged in the first place! Forgiveness frees you from the tangles of anger and retribution, and from preoccupations with the past and the case in your mind about another person. As you forgive, your own deep and natural goodness is increasingly revealed.

How

You do not *have* to forgive anyone. If forgiveness is forced or grudging or inauthentic, it's not really forgiveness. Sometimes we're just not ready to forgive. It may be too soon or what happened could be unforgivable. Don't let other people push you into a forgiveness that is not genuine for you. If you have an intuition that you could indeed forgive someone but somewhere inside there's a block to doing that, try to explore the block. Perhaps it's telling you that you need to learn more about the other person's motives before you can move on or that you need to let yourself be really angry about what they did to you. You can take your time to decide whether you want to move into forgiveness. And when you do, try the suggestions below.

Take Care of Yourself

It's hard to forgive while you're feeling overwhelmed or if you're being actively mistreated. Do what you can to protect yourself and others. Repair the damage as best you can, and resize the relationship if need be. Keep making your life a good one. You can forgive people while shrinking, if not ending, your relationship with them.

Ask for Support

It is usually easier to forgive someone if others stand with you in recognizing the ways you've been mistreated. Those who support you may be able to do nothing about what has happened, but just knowing that they see what you see and that they care about you can help immensely.

Let Yourself Feel It

Forgiveness is not about shutting down your emotional reactions. Allow your thoughts and feelings and desires to have breathing room, to ebb and flow over time with their own natural rhythms. Opening to the whole of your experience in a big space of mindful awareness can help you come to a sense of completion and resolution *for yourself* about what happened—which is good in its own right, and an aid to forgiveness.

Check Your Story

Watch out for exaggerating how awful, significant, or unforgivable something is. Be careful about making assumptions about the intentions of others (chapter 20, "Take It Less Personally"). With modern life, many of us are pretty stressed and scatterbrained much of the time, and maybe you, unfortunately, just bumped into someone's bad day. Put the event in perspective: Was it really that big a deal? Maybe it was, but maybe it wasn't.

Appreciate the Value of Forgiveness

Ask yourself: *What do my grievances, my reproaches, cost me? What do they cost others I care about? What would it be like to lay down those burdens?*

Consider where your self-interest really lies. Imagine that your indignation, outrage, and resentment are like stones you're carrying. Notice how heavy they are . . . and then imagine tossing them into the sea. How would that feel?

See the Big Picture

Consider the many factors upstream from the people who've hurt you, such as their childhood, parents, finances, temperament, health, and so on. This is not to minimize what they did or to overlook their responsibility, but to place it in a larger context *for your sake.* When you see some of the many forces bearing down on others, you can understand their actions more objectively, which can help to lessen their sting, even if you continue to disapprove of them. Try to see the many things about your life—in the present, in the past, and looking ahead toward the future—that are good and untouched by what the other person did.

Accept That Life Is Wounding

There's a Zen story in which Master Yunmen is asked: *How is it when the tree withers and the leaves fall?* He replies: *Body exposed in the golden wind.*

There are depths in this teaching that I'm still exploring. One thing does seem clear: To enjoy the golden winds of all that is good in our relationships, we must live exposed . . . including to injury. We all get wounded, one way or another. We're big monkeys, not long out of the trees. People sometimes do crappy things. This is not to excuse it, but to recognize the reality of it. Sometimes people will treat you unjustly and get away with it. It's wrong, but we all face it. Seen in this way, it's not so personal. It's life, it's living and working with other human beings. We can both stand up to mistreatment and have a sense of perspective about it when it happens.

Tell Yourself—and Maybe Them

When you feel ready to forgive someone, you could say it to yourself and see how it feels. For example: *I forgive you . . . I'm letting go of this . . . I still think it was wrong, but I'm not going to let it bother me any more.* Find the words that feel genuine for you.

And then, if you like, tell them. Hopefully, they'll be receptive. And, if not, you can still have the benefits of forgiveness inside your own heart—while now seeing that other person even more clearly.

Part Six

Love the World

47

Love What's Real

As I grew up, my family and my schools felt like shaky ground. I didn't understand why my parents and many kids so often reacted in the ways they did, with big anger or fear to seemingly small events. It felt shaky inside me, too, and I didn't understand my own feelings and reactions. Outside and inside both felt twirly, up in the air, unnerving.

So I looked for solid ground. I tried to see and understand what was really true. The orange groves and hills around our home were natural and comforting, and I went there whenever I could. I started reading science fiction and liked an orderly universe in which you could figure out why the spaceship didn't work and fix it.

I also tried to figure out what was real inside other people, and myself. *Why is my mom so cranky? Oh, she's mad at my dad. Why is this bully picking on me? Oh, he's trying to look big in front of his friends. Why does that girl look so hurt? Oh, it's because I did something mean. Why do I feel shy in groups? Oh, I'm afraid they'll make fun of what I say.*

Years later, the real is my primary touchstone and refuge. Sure, mysteries remain, and our descriptions of what's real are incomplete and shaped by culture. Still, there is a *lot* that we *can* know about—from microbes in your gut and feelings in your mind to a ripple in space-time caused by two black holes crashing together.

Besides knowing what's real, we can *love* it as well, gobsmacked by its existence, reassured by seeing clearly rather than being tricked or deluded. We don't have to like what's real to love its realness.

What's the one thing that *unhealthy* individuals, couples, families, organizations, and governments all have in common? They hide, distort, or attack the real truth of things. For example, "family secrets" are classic signs of trouble, in which good stories—*Oh, Mom doesn't drink that much . . . Oh, Uncle Bob isn't creepy, he's just affectionate*—hide bad facts.

On the other hand, what's the one thing that *healthy* individuals, couples, families, organizations, and governments all have in common? They are grounded in what is real. They seek the truth and help others find it themselves. They tell the truth, and they deal with it as best they can.

How

I like to start with physical objects, such as a stone in the hand, water in a cup, or book on a table. Let your perceptions move from object to object, seen or heard or touched or imagined—one after another, all real . . . extending to the hand holding the stone and the brain constructing the sensations of its shape and texture: It is all real! For a few breaths or longer, be aware of one real thing after another: plants and animals, forks and spoons, earth and sky, stars above and worms below . . . so many real things. If you relax and open into this, a kind of wild ecstasy can bubble up, and gratitude and awe.

We are each supported by countless real things. For example, while sitting, standing, or walking, be aware of how your bones are holding you up. Shift your posture until you feel firmly supported, with a sense of uprightness and strength. Really register this whole experience of very physical support. You can see many things that protect, aid, or delight you, from sturdy walls and electric lights to flowers in a vase or a picture of a friend. You could bring to mind someone who supports you, and take a moment to feel the realness of this person, and the realness of their support for you. As you face life's challenges—including people who are not supportive—it's important to appreciate real support where you can find it.

Whatever you find sacred is real. It could be related to religion or spirituality, or to anything you cherish, such as old-growth redwoods, the light in a child's eyes, or the inherent goodness in the human heart. If you're like me, you don't stay continually aware of what's most dear to you. But when you come back to it—perhaps at a wedding or a funeral, or standing at the edge of the sea—there's a sense of coming home, of "yes," of knowing that *this* really matters and deserves your love.

Loving what's real is a fundamental thankfulness that *you* exist and that *anything* exists at all. There is an accepting, a humility, a respect. Many things that are real are stressful or unjust. We would not wish them upon others, and don't want them for ourselves—yet we can still love the real everything that includes these particular things.

Loving what's real makes it easier to see what you may tend to turn away from, such as facts about your health, finances, or relationships, or what is happening down in the basement of your own mind. You might consider, as I am lately, the real effects adding up of compassion or anger toward others, and the real choices about how best to use the remaining years and days of this life. Can you use a love of the real to face and deal with something that's important?

One way to love what's real is to listen or look for it coming to

262 Making Great Relationships

you from others. How are your friends or family really doing inside? What do they need? Where does it hurt? Much as our own experiences are real to us, their experiences are keenly, sometimes painfully, real to *them*. You can feel the weight of their inner world. Even if you don't exactly like what might be streaming along in someone's consciousness, you can bow to its realness—which will bring you a greater sense of ease about it.

Whether it's in our families or our countries, telling the truth—and supporting others who do the same—is an active and courageous way to love what's real. Sometimes this may not be safe, such as with governments that punish open dissent. And sometimes it may not be appropriate, such as not wanting to burden aging parents with the full truth of their impact on you as a child. But you can always tell *yourself* the truth inside the sanctuary of your own mind.

The real is our precious refuge. It's what we can count on. Including the real goodness inside each one of us. The real good wishes for others, the real efforts each day, the real inherent wakefulness. You can love what's real in *you*, and in that love find an opening into all that is real everywhere.

48

Take Heart

By *taking heart*, I mean several related things:

- Sensing your heart and chest
- Finding encouragement in all that is good
- Resting in your own warmth, compassion, and kindness; resting in the caring for you from others; love flowing in and love flowing out
- Being courageous, wholehearted, and stronghearted; going forward wisely even when you're anxious, knowing your own truth and, as much as you can, speaking it

When you take heart, you're better able to deal with challenges like aging, illness, trauma, or conflicts with others. You're also better able to take advantage of opportunities with confidence and grit.

It takes heart to live in even ordinary times. And it particularly takes heart to live in, live with, and live beyond really hard times. Your personal hard time might be bad news about your health, the death of a parent, or betrayal by others. Or it could be related to changes in your country and your world, and your concerns about their effects on others and yourself.

There are so many examples of honorable people facing great difficulty with dignity, principle, and courage. They did it. We can, too.

How

Start by riding out the storm. When big things happen—whether in a child's schoolyard or in a refugee camp on the other side of the world—it is natural to be shocked and disturbed by them. It helps to stay with the raw experience, the body sensations, the deep feelings, the stirred-up fears and anger—rather than spinning out into obsessive thinking. Whatever it is, it is *your* experience, and it's OK if you're more affected by it than some other people. You can be mindful of what is passing through the big open space of awareness, observing it without being flooded by it.

When the bottom falls out, do simple things that help you come back to center and find your footing. For example, make your bed or call a friend. Take good care of your body by making a nice meal for yourself and trying to get enough sleep. Take some deep breaths and perhaps meditate a bit. When it's true, notice that you're basically all right in the present—still breathing, heart still beating, not completely overwhelmed—in this moment, moment after moment. Find a little pleasure somewhere, perhaps the smell of an orange or the feeling of warm water on your face. Look at trees and sky, get a cup of tea and stare into space.

Guard and guide your attention. It's one thing to find facts and form the best plans you can. It's another thing to get distracted or upset by news or other people that do not add any useful value to your life.

Take heart in so much that is good. Outside you, there is the kindness in others, the beauty of a single leaf, the stars that still shine no matter what hides them. Right now, as you read, all over the world children are laughing in delight, families are sitting down to a meal, babies are being born, and loving arms are holding people who are dying. Inside you, there is your compassion, sincere efforts, happy memories, capabilities—and much more.

Take heart with others, sharing worries, support, and friendship.

Do the things you can. The more that events are turbulent, alarming, and beyond your control, the more important it is to focus on stability, safety, and agency in any ways that are available to you.

Have courage. Strong forces have always tried to confuse and frighten others. Meanwhile, you can preserve an inner strength, never cowed or bowed in your core.

Last, I've found it really helps to have perspective. Without minimizing one bit of anything that's awful, it is also true that humans like you and me have been on our planet for 300,000 years. I see the trees, the land, the ocean—all of it here before me and lasting long after me. Empires rise and fall. Sometimes the center does not hold—in a body, a marriage, or a nation—and still. And still people love each other, go out of their way for a stranger, and marvel at a rainbow. Nothing, *nothing* at all can change this. We keep putting one foot in front of the other one, lifting each other up along the way.

49

Vote

E ven in a world with billions of people, what we do affects each other, for better or worse. We are connected with every other human being. In a book about how we respond to and treat others, it's appropriate to consider our political relationships in the societies that we share. How we govern ourselves might seem abstract and remote, but its consequences are intimate and personal.

You might be worried about the economy, the storms and droughts of climate change, or new diseases spreading across the globe. You might be alarmed by the rise of authoritarianism around the world. You might be appalled, as I am here in America, by the long history of slavery, racism, and social injustice. You might be deeply concerned about the world that our children and theirs will inherit.

When certain things happen, such as the murder of a Black man by a white police officer, it's natural to feel stunned, shocked, powerless. And to be flooded with outrage or an overwhelming sorrow. Still, even in the midst of all this, you can be mindful—aware and present, and not entirely swept away. Then at some point you take a breath and look around and try to figure out what to do.

One thing to do is to *vote*. We vote in lots of ways. Besides what we do at the ballot box, we offer a kind of vote—a choice with consequences—when we sign a petition or send money to a cause or a candidate. In a broad sense, we vote when we speak up for anyone who is being mistreated. Inside your mind, you cast a kind of vote when you take a moral stand. The root of the word *vote* is *vow*: to make a commitment, to claim the power you do have—and use it.

Someone might say, *It doesn't matter. Any single vow, any single vote, is a drop in the ocean.*

But every choice matters to the person who makes it. Knowing that you are committed to something and have kept your word to yourself, that you've walked your talk, feels good in its own right. Plus, it's a powerful antidote to helplessness and despair.

Further, when others see you taking action, that can inspire them to do the same. And the gradual accumulation of many little efforts, drop by drop, can become a mighty stream. I came of age in the late 1960s, and in my lifetime I've seen major improvements in civil rights, environmentalism, gay marriage, and women's rights. These changes have been the result of countless "votes" that have added up over time.

We still have a long way to go. The votes we cast—with our ballots and words and deeds—are no guarantee of success. But if we don't vote, again and again, what's guaranteed is failure.

How

Vote for Facts

Being foggy about facts is like driving a car with your eyes closed. Some say that we can't really know the truth about big things like national governments or climate change. I think that's lazy, at best. The basics are usually pretty easy to see. Who's getting richer and who's getting poorer? Are glaciers melting? Who's strengthening democracy, and who's weakening it? Ten or twenty minutes online with some credible sources will tell you a lot, particularly when they are consistent with each other. Depending on the issue, you can find good summaries for the general public from university institutes, scientific and professional organizations, nonpartisan nonprofits, Wikipedia, and major news organizations, such as the BBC and the *New York Times*. These sources are not perfect, but what makes them credible is that they compete with each other for accuracy and when they fall short, they make corrections.

We are intimately affected by real events, both in the hallways of our homes and in the halls of power. When someone tells you, *Don't worry. You don't need to know the truth, you don't need to worry about that* . . . you usually do. People who lie in order to hold on to their authority delegitimize it. Any person, group, or government that says facts are irrelevant, or makes it harder to find them, or spews disinformation to crowd out the truth, is attacking the foundation of all healthy relationships.

Turn in Your Ballot

Voting is about participation—and *participation itself is not partisan*. In US presidential elections, about two in five people do not bother to vote—and young people, eighteen- to twenty-five-year-olds, are even less engaged, although they will most inherit the effects of global warming, wealth inequality, and other serious social problems. Voting is sacred. As Representative John Lewis wrote a few days before he died: "Democracy is not a state. It is an act."

Confront Bad Faith

It's one thing to argue about politics in good faith. Then there is a shared interest in the actual facts, and if *you* shouldn't do something, well, *I* shouldn't do it, either. As we've seen, telling the truth and playing fair are the foundation of all relationships—from two people in a couple to millions of people in a country. Lying and cheating are not tolerated in sports or business. So why do we put up with them in our politics?

What you do will depend on the situation. You might ignore some troll on Facebook, or gently ask a friend with different views if you could talk about politics in another kind of way.

Or as soon as it's clear that the other person has zero interest in a good faith dialogue, you might say something like this: *What's your real purpose here? You keep saying things that are untrue or are unrelated to what I'm talking about. You're just trying to change the subject, instead of dealing with what I'm saying.* Even if you don't get anywhere with that person, you've stopped wasting your time, plus you might have a good effect on others who are watching.

Stand Up for Others

I remember being ten years old and the visceral shock of going to a gas station's bathroom in North Carolina in 1963 and seeing three doors labeled: Men . . . Women . . . Colored. My life has had its difficulties, but as a white man I've been advantaged in many ways. I look at my home and my savings, and know they are the result of three kinds of things: personal efforts, luck (good or bad, including the genetic lottery), and advantages that operate *by disadvantaging others*. Some fraction of what I own comes from current and historical discrimination against women, people of color, and other marginalized groups. That fraction is not 100 percent, but it's certainly not 0 percent. Whatever it is, it's ill-gotten gains.

Most people don't walk out the front door planning to disadvantage others. This is about sorrow, not shame, and compassion and a commitment to justice. For those of us who have benefited, as I have, from systemic advantages, I think we have a particular responsibility to do what we can. As we vote with our thoughts and words, we can listen, and feel the weight of what's being said, and try to learn and not assume, and recognize impacts on others (regardless of what our intent may have been), and find the sincere desire to be an ally, and keep trying to be a better one. As we vote at the ballot box, we can choose politicians and policies that protect the youngest among us, that address racial inequities, and that create opportunities for every single one of us.

Vote for Yourself

Deep down, we each have the power to see what we see, value what we value, and make our own plans. It may not be safe or useful to say this out loud. But we can always say it to ourselves.

That's a kind of vote. No matter what happens out there in the world, we can always vote within our own minds. It's like we each have an inner voting booth. We can take refuge in the sure knowing of what we do there.

I draw guidance and strength from people who have faced vastly greater hardships than I have, and who speak of what we can do inside ourselves with the authority of their own suffering and pain. Most of these people are not famous, and still their words have tremendous weight. Some are well known, such as the

Dalai Lama. I remember watching an interview with him in which he described the terrible mistreatment of Tibetans in their own country. In his face and tone and words, he expressed that irreducible human freedom to make our own choices, to claim the power that we do have, and to use it—and use it well—with compassion for all beings.

Cherish the Earth

Our brain has three primary motivational systems—avoiding harms, approaching rewards, and attaching to those we care about—that draw on many neural networks to accomplish their goals. Lately, I've started to realize that a fourth motivational system might be emerging as well.

Our hunter-gatherer ancestors did not have much capacity for harming their world, nor could they have much understanding of their effects on it. But now, humanity has vast powers to help and to hurt. And we have inescapable knowledge of what we are doing to our own home. Eight billion of us are pressing hard against the limits of Lifeboat Earth. As the planet heats up, as many species become extinct, and as resources such as fresh water decline, for our own species to survive and to flourish, cultural and perhaps biological evolution might be calling us to *cherish the earth*.

This is the most fundamental relationship of all, the one between each of us and the earth we share. I feel it's fitting that we explore it in the last chapter of this book.

How

The world is near at hand in the food you eat, the air you breathe, and the weather and climate in which you spend your days. In widening circles, it includes complex webs of life in the land, the sea, and the sky. When we cherish the earth, we both *appreciate* it and *care* for it.

So look for opportunities to enjoy and value different things in the natural world. These range from what is close by—flowers blooming, trees offering shade, honeybees moving from plant to plant—to the vast nest we all share, such as the exchanges of oxygen and carbon dioxide through which animals and plants give breath to each other. We can appreciate the fortuitous occurrence of our rocky planet surviving the early formation of a solar system to find an orbit that allows for liquid water on its surface . . . and the even more remarkable occurrence of this universe bubbling into being: the largest nest of all, the extraordinary miracle in which we make our ordinary days.

You could look for ways to protect and nurture our vulnerable and precious world. We're all involved with systems of extraction and pollution, and with the heavy boot of humanity on countless other species. No one can do everything, but everyone can do something. Pick something that matters to you, perhaps eating less meat or none at all, turning off lights when you're not using them, or spending about a dollar a day on projects that offset the CO_2 that your activities send up into the sky. Plant a tree, recycle when you can, and support people and political parties that are serious about capping and eventually reversing global warming.

At the heart of it, what is our relationship with this planet? Do we relate to it as an object to be exploited, an adversary, or a distant acquaintance? Or do we cherish it as a friend, a fragile sanctuary, a beloved home?

Here and there and everywhere, let's all live in a world we love.

Acknowledgments

We learn something about relationships from everyone we've had a relationship with, so I fear it's impossible for me to acknowledge all of them adequately. I'll simply say that my wife and children have been my greatest teachers.

I've also learned a lot from dear friends, including Adhimutti Bhikkhuni, Peter Baumann, Stuart Bell, Tom Bowlin, Tara Brach, John Casey, Caren Cole, Mark Coleman, Andy Dreitcer, Daniel Ellenberg, Pam Handleman, John Kleiner, Marc Lesser, Roddy McCalley, Rick Mendius, John Prendergast, Henry Shukman, Michael Taft, and Bob Truog. When I was a shy and awkward undergrad at UCLA, several mentors were crucial, notably Carol Hetrick, Chuck Rusch, Mike Van Horn, and Jules Zentner.

The field of psychology has explored relationships in depth, and in this book I've drawn on attachment theory, family systems theory, and nonviolent communication—as well as on my thirty-five years of doing therapy with individuals and couples. I am deeply grateful to everyone who ever trusted me enough as a counselor to come speak with me. There is also a great deal of practical wisdom in the contemplative traditions, including in the one I know best, early Buddhism. Leslie Booker and Mamphela Ramphele have helped me be more aware of my privilege and bias, and more skillful in how I communicate.

This book draws on some of the short essays in my free weekly newsletter, *Just One Thing*. Over the years I've received helpful comments from many readers—thank you!

Charlotte Nuessle gave the book a helpful read, and of course my patient and wise editor, Donna Loffredo, made many invaluable suggestions and corrections. Diana Drew provided meticulous copyediting, and the whole group at Penguin Random House has truly been a joy to work with. Throughout, my friend and agent Amy Rennert has guided me with her wonderful blend of kindness and expertise. Our team at Being Well, Inc., led by Stephanie Veillon, includes Forrest Hanson, Michelle Keane, Sui Oakland, Paul Van de Riet, Marion Reynolds, and Andrew Schuman—and you've been making great relationships with me and each other from the first day you started!

Thank you, each of you. And may our sincere efforts foster a world in which we can all live together in peace.

Index

Rick Hanson, PhD, is a psychologist, senior fellow at UC Berkeley's Greater Good Science Center, and *New York Times* bestselling author. His seven books have been published in thirty languages and include *Buddha's Brain, Making Great Relationships, Neurodharma, Resilient, Hardwiring Happiness, Just One Thing,* and *Mother Nurture*—with over a million copies in English alone. His free newsletters have 250,000 subscribers, and his online programs have scholarships available for those with financial need. Hosted with his son Forrest, their Being Well podcast is downloaded several million times each year. He has lectured at NASA, Google, Oxford, and Harvard, and has taught in meditation centers worldwide. An expert on positive neuroplasticity, his work has been featured on CBS, NPR, the BBC, and other major media; his paper "Learning to Learn from Positive Experiences" was recently published in the *Journal of Positive Psychology.* He began meditating in 1974 and is the founder of the Wellspring Institute for Neuroscience and Contemplative Wisdom. He and his wife live in northern California and have two adult children. He loves the wilderness and taking a break from emails.

Also by *New York Times* bestselling author
RICK HANSON, PhD

Seven practices for strengthening the neural circuitry of profound contentment and inner peace.

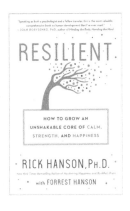

A practical guide to developing the twelve inner strengths of lasting well-being in a challenging world.

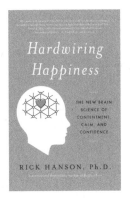

Counterbalance your brain's negativity bias and learn to hardwire happiness in only a few minutes each day.

HARMONY
BOOKS

Available wherever books are sold